T0129277

SCARLET ROSE

a novel

Antonio F. Vianna

authorHOUSE®

AuthorHouse™
1663 Liberty Drive
Bloomington, IN 47403
www.authorhouse.com
Phone: 1-800-839-8640

Published by AuthorHouse 1/9/2013

ISBN: 978-1-4817-0577-6 (sc)
ISBN: 978-1-4817-0576-9 (e)

Library of Congress Control Number: 2013900300

ACKNOWLEDGEMENT

This book has been masterfully edited by Jessica Smith. Her enduring patience and skillful contributions are what every writer needs.

AUTHOR'S INITIAL REMARKS

Temptations are everywhere and everyone is tempted at least once in their life to do something they know is wrong. The story is about uncontrolled temptations and how easy it is to repeat the lure again and again until it becomes a habit that is difficult to break. Charles and Cass Westfield are otherwise ordinary people who are bound and determined to keep her most precious secrets hidden from one another and their daughter, Scarlet Rose. They are willing to pay the emotional price for being pulled into their own temptations.

Chapter 1

A 37-year-old woman sits outside a local cafe. Her back is to a light-colored coarse wall that acts to contrast with her smooth golden-brown skin. The sun strikes her face just in the right way to accentuate pronounced cheek bones. Her five feet-seven inch trim body fidgets in the chair. She is agitated as she looks around. Cass Westfield is expecting a close friend to talk over something important, something she is not sure her husband would understand, more of a woman-topic. She takes a small sip of coffee but does not recognize the taste since she is preoccupied with something more important. A cool breeze tosses her short brown hair slightly into the air. Dark sunglasses block the anxiousness in her deep brown eyes. She gets jumpier as seconds tick away. She wonders how long she will need to wait before her friend shows up. She is about to text another message, but then she spots Iris. Immediately the strain in her face lessens. She sets the coffee cup on top of the black metal table and calls out. "Over here!" Cass waves towards Iris. "I'm over here!" She pinches her lips tightly together.

Iris is the same age as Cass. Her shinny long black hair

that is pulled back provides a sharp distinction to her close friend. Her long slender legs gracefully pick up the pace to find out what is troubling Cass. Iris waves back. She forces a smile to conceal worry about her dear friend.

Before Iris is able to take her seat, Cass says, "Here, I bought you a latte." Cass moves the cup closer to Iris as her friend pulls the chair away from the table to sit. "I'm so glad you're here." Her voice quivers slightly.

"I came as quick as I could." Iris is slightly out of breath. "Your text sounded urgent." She removes her sunglasses. Her dark eyes stare towards Cass, unblinking. "There must be something wrong" She sits in the empty chair, not interested at the moment in the beverage. She swallows, wonders what is so important.

"You're such a dear friend. I can always count on you." Cass pats Iris' hand. "Thanks for coming on such a short notice."

"Yes, yes, don't worry about that." Iris pauses and then continues. "What's this about?"

Cass looks away, and tips her head downward.

"Are you and Charles splitting up?"

Cass turns to face Iris and then straightens her body. She is surprised. "Why would you say that?"

"Please. Unless you've been making up a bunch of stories, what else should I think?" Iris cocks her head to the side and then she clarifies. "He's been out of work for some time now. You've told me he's grumpy all the time, not to mention any sex in your life, and he's driving you so crazy that you've become a work-alcoholic." She stares at Cass as if her answer is intuitively obvious.

Cass turns away again and then resets her face towards Iris. "No, we're not separating or anything like that."

"Then what's it about?"

She smiles. "I've made a decision about something." Her voice is now resolved and upbeat with enthusiasm, a quick change from just seconds ago.

Iris frowns as she waits for her friend to continue. The pause in conversation enables her to take a sip of latte and then to return the cup to the black metal table top. "OK, are you going to tell me, or is this a guessing game?"

Cass clears her throat as if she is about to lecture to an audience. She takes in a deep breath of air and slowly lets it escape. "Remember when I told you I wasn't going to my class reunion?"

Iris nods, yes, but the frown on her face says something else. She is confused about the importance of a class reunion. "I thought that was all settled, but go on." She shrugs her shoulders.

"Well, I've changed my mind." Cass settles back into her chair. A slight smile creases her face. "I'm going to attend. It's final."

Creases appear on Iris' forehead, now doubly unsure of the importance of the decision. "I don't get it. Is that why you asked me here, to tell me you're now going to your class reunion?" She shakes her head sideways, puzzled.

Cass smirks as if she is about to say something mischievous.

Iris pushes for an answer. "Enlighten me."

"I leave in two days. I can't wait." There is definite excitement in her voice. "I haven't seen anyone for quite a while. It's going to be great!"

Iris remains baffled. She senses her body tense up a bit and a thin film of anger inside rising. She remains confused about the urgency of the meeting. "There's more to this, you can't fool me." Iris' stare is intense.

Cass places her sunglasses on the table. Her eyes are wider than normal without saying a word. She feels all wound up in side.

Iris continues. "I still don't get it. Is Charles going with you?"

"No, he's not interested." Her voice settles down a wee bit but her look remains enthused. "He thinks reunions only get people depressed. He's staying home."

Iris still is baffled why her friend seemed so desperate to talk with her, yet she goes along with Cass' conversation. She wills herself to relax. "Too bad, they can be a lot of fun if you have the right attitude."

Cass is too animated to notice Iris' puzzlement. "Yeah, I agree." She grins. "It's all in the attitude."

Iris takes a small sip of latte. "There's more. Come on, what really is happening?"

She leans closer to Iris as if she is about to let on a big secret. "You won't believe whom I heard from." Cass' voice is drenched with excitement.

"I'm waiting." Iris pauses, "Come on, tell me, who was it?" She slowly gets inspired to listen to more.

"I got an e-mail from someone whom I haven't seen or heard from in a while." She is all wound up with enthusiasm.

"I hope I'm not going to hear what I think you're about to say."

"What's that supposed to mean?"

"I'll wait to hear from you first, go on."

"He used to make me laugh." Cass pauses and takes a deep swallow. "I can't believe I feel so young again."

Iris cautions her friend, "It's what I thought you'd say."

"Don't look so worried."

"It's not me whom I'm worried about."

Cass frowns. "You're worried about me, what for?"

Iris explains. "You're getting all worked up over him. Remember, you're a married woman."

Cass puckers her lips. "I know that. You don't have to remind me." However, at the same time, Cass' eyes tell another story.

Iris shakes her head, doubtful that this is all there is to it. "Tell me about him, what was so special about this guy?"

Cass is still keyed up. She speaks rapidly without taking a single breath. "He was tall, probably a little over six feet, brown eyes, black curly hair, and olive complexion. He had the best smile ever. The first time we met during a freshman mixer we were attracted to each other."

"That was a long time ago."

"Yeah, I know, but I still feel it."

Iris is more worried about her friend being so ecstatic, yet she asks, "He sounds like a winner. Why didn't the two of you marry?"

Cass pauses before she answers. A slight frown wrinkles her otherwise smooth forehead. "Good question." She looks away as if to hide from telling the truth. "You know, just one of those things."

"That's a code word we women use to hide something. What else?"

Cass briefly stops talking as her mind spins back in time. Then she continues to talk as if no one is around. "He had a private side about him, something that he kept hidden all the time." Slowly she changes around to face Iris. A look of surprise covers her face as if it is the first time she recognizes that Iris is sitting across from her. "It sort of scared me and excited me at the same time. Everyone who knew him felt the same way. No one asked." She takes another pause to think about those college days.

Iris is now fully convinced she hasn't heard the full story and wonders if she should ask a few questions. At minimum she does not believe her friend is doing the right thing by attending the class reunion alone. She hesitates before saying anything further. Then she puts that worry aside for the moment to pry a bit further, "Hmm. What else?" She does not spend a long time to wait for Cass' reply. Iris gets to the point quickly. "But something happened between the two of you, didn't it."

"Why are you asking that?"

"Because something did happen."

Cass ignores the question, still dwelling on something else. "Mike, that's his name, was from Hoboken, New Jersey."

Iris narrows her eyes. She does not understand the importance of where he was born. "And the meaning of that is?"

Cass wants to reminisce about his background so she ignores the question. "There was a guy hanging around Mike most of the time. I don't think he was a student because I never saw him in class, but to be honest, I don't really know. The guy looked like he was only a few years older than Mike. He was huge in size, not in height but in weight. I'd put him at a few inches less than six feet but well over two hundred solid pounds. I never heard him say one word or even smile. He was just there. I remember asking Mike one time about who the guy was but Mike said he was just someone his family wanted to be nearby." She squirms in her chair.

Iris' eyes widen. It is not the answer she expected. "Come on, you know what this sounds like?"

"Huh?"

"This sounds like the Mafia!"

"Oh, no."

"Oh, yes. You were dating a Mafia son!"

Iris' response spotlights something important. Cass gets back into a two-way conversation. She waves her hand to push off the idea. "I don't think so. He was one of the kindest people I knew at that time, usually soft spoken and real sweet. No, I can't imagine any Mafia connection." She glances away at nothing in particular.

Iris knows there is more to come so she patiently waits to hear the rest of Cass' story.

Cass continues. "But, sometimes he'd get real angry over little things, his temper would flare unexpectedly. He said he liked everything perfect." She smiles, "Yeah that was Mike, wanting everything done perfectly and his own way."

"You weren't afraid of him?"

"Oh no, I knew how to handle him. He listened to me. I knew how to cool him down."

"What's his full name?"

"Mike Aviara."

Iris chuckles. "Duh."

"What does that mean?"

"Cass, come on, what do you think it means? Aviara? His last name ends in a vowel. Duh?"

"I think you've watched the Godfather too many times."

"Have it your way." Iris shrugs her shoulders. She accepts for the time being that whatever else is on Cass' mind will not be revealed now. Iris continues in the same vein of discussion. "So what did Mike say in the e-mail?"

Cass' voice returns to a high pitch signaling excitement. She is ready for a two way dialog. "He wanted to know if I was going to the reunion."

"And you said yes."

"I didn't say yes at first."

"But you changed your mind, why?"

"He said that maybe we could get together for old times."

Iris shakes her head, no, "Bad idea."

"Why?"

"If you ask me, I think it's too much of a temptation."

"Come on, he's just a college friend whom I haven't seen in years."

"I'd think you'd be more cautious since you seemed nervous and anxious when you talked about the guy who hung around Mike in college."

"That was a long time ago."

Iris takes another point of view. "Would you get together with Mike if Charles were with you?"

Cass keeps quiet, yet she knows the truth.

Iris flickers her eyebrows. "Do I have to say anything further?" She pauses and then continues. "But I know you will attend anyway, so please listen. If your husband finds out about this, he'll go ballistic. You and Charles should try to work out whatever problems you're having. It's best that way."

"I never said anything about problems between Charles and me."

"You didn't have to. You're easy to read."

"There are no problems between us."

"Honestly?"

Cass pauses before she goes on. "You and I both know how stubborn Charles is. He's been unemployed for over six months and doesn't want to do anything except mope around the house." A flood of disclosure flows out of her mouth that she cannot seem to stop. "We used to go out to dinner a couple times a week, take in a movie, and take off on short weekend trips. That's all disappeared. He no longer has any interest in me. I mean, I try to get him aroused in bed, but he just turns to his side and complains he's tired. I think I'm going mad. Sometimes it doesn't even feel as if we are married."

Iris reaches to place her hand over her friend's hand. "I'm sure that will work its way out. Just have some more patience and don't do anything foolish."

"Who says I'm doing anything foolish?"

"Be honest. What if Charles finds out that you've spent time with an old flame during the reunion? What then?"

"Who said Mike was an old flame? He's just someone whom I haven't seen since college?" She crosses her arms.

Iris smirks. "Who are you trying to fool? Come on, you're flirting with danger, and you know it." She nods her head sideways, "Don't do it. It's not worth it."

Cass' eyes are the desperate looking type. "I'm 37

years old and I'm not getting any younger. I'm not going to do anything foolish, but I've got needs too."

"And something inside you got all heated up when you read his e-mail."

"Yes! I even saw his face and heard his voice in my head. It was as if we were still in college." Cass breaths in and out quickly.

"That's exactly what I mean."

Cass keeps quiet.

"You haven't gotten over him, and now is not the time to rekindle the relationship."

"You keep saying more than what there really is. He's just someone whom I haven't seen in years."

"Did you sleep with him in college?"

Cass clears her throat and tightens her lips more firmly together.

Iris knows she is onto learning the truth so she continues, "I take that as a yes. How often?"

"What is this, an investigation? I know what I'm doing."

"So, I guess it was several times. He must have been good, real good." Iris flickers her eyebrows. "Did you and he do anything kinky?"

"What makes you think I'm the kinky type?"

"I'm just asking. I don't know. Did you?"

"Iris, you're creating something out of nothing."

"Cass, then why did you text me if you didn't want to talk about it?" She waits for Cass to answer but there is only silence. Iris continues. "You're looking for someone to please you, no matter if you are happily married or not. It happens to many women our age, but it doesn't have to happen at all. I think it's as simple as that."

Cass hesitates, reluctant to say anything immediately. She gives herself time to think. "You're my best friend. I can say anything to you. I feel safe in talking with you."

"I feel the same about you. Is something else bothering you and do you want to tell me?"

Cass takes a deep swallow. "I'm concerned about Charles' mental state." She refocuses on Iris. "I've read up about it, and we've talked about it a little, but not much."

Iris is taken by surprise of the change in topic. "Oh." She stares directly at Cass. "Go on, I'm listening."

Cass clears her throat. The first few words are unsteady. "Have you heard of people who have sleep terrors?"

"I know of sleepwalking but I've never heard of sleep terrors. Are they the same?"

"No, they are quite different."

Is that what Charles has, sleep terrors?"

"Yes, at least I think so, but I'm not one hundred percent certain." Cass takes in a deep and labored breath of air. Nothing comes out of her mouth at first. Then she exhales before she says, "I've done some research on this through the Internet."

Iris shoves her chair closer to Cass. "Go on, I'm listening. Talk as slowly as you want. I'm here."

Cass continues. "Sleepwalking usually happens when people leave their beds and start acting out dreams. Lots of people sleepwalk but few people have sleep terrors." There is fright all over her face, but she manages to continue. "Sleep terrors often turn up with people who are sleepwalkers after they experience something devastating in their lives, like a death of a loved one or a near fatal incident themselves. These people act out their worst

11

nightmares, and when they wake up they have very little to no recollection. If they remember anything, it's just the image or emotion of doom and fear, the need to defend themselves from someone or something. I've read where people have killed their spouses during a sleep terror and have no memory of what happened."

Iris interrupts, "Are you afraid that Charles might kill you? Is that what you're saying?"

"No." She pauses and then changes her mind. "Yes." Another hesitation, "Maybe, I really don't know what I'm saying! Charles is prone to sleepwalking. That's something he's done most of his life. But since he lost his job he is more worried than I've ever seen. It is as if he is grieving over losing the job and can't find another one to replace it. I'm worried the sleepwalking might become sleep terrors." Cass is frantic.

"That sounds like a big jump for Charles, from sleepwalking to sleep terrors. Do you think you might be overreacting?" Iris stays calm.

"Maybe, but his employment situation is sure taking its toll on me."

"I think you should talk with him about it to let him know how worried you are and how it is affecting you."

"I've tried but he doesn't want to talk about it. He just gets upset when I bring it up. No, I'm not going to do anything. I just hope he finds a job sooner than later."

Iris shakes her head sideways. "Take him to a doctor or the both of you go to a counselor. This seems to be worrying you a lot."

Cass' voice quivers. "No, he wouldn't go. He'd just deny everything."

"OK, but you're really upset about it. I think you should do something, if just for yourself."

Cass' face is without expression.

"So, when you heard from Mike you felt better, is that it?"

Cass gets out of her self-imposed trance, and lets a puff of air out of her mouth. "Yeah, I guess so. I'm so at a loss at how to help Charles. And then, all of a sudden, when Mike unexpectedly reappeared, I felt alive again."

"Like you were back in college."

"Yeah, back in college."

"I still don't think you should see Mike from Hoboken."

"Maybe I don't know much about anything these days. Maybe I'm confused and just need to get away for a while to recharge my batteries."

"Don't make that an excuse to see Mike."

Cass stares at Iris without a reply.

"How's Scarlet Rose doing?"

At the sound of her daughter's voice, Cass' face turns bright. She turns to face Iris. "She's doing great at school, a straight-A-student. But she very much wants to be sixteen years old. That's an important age for girls these days. I keep telling her she has to wait one more year, there's nothing she can do to make it happen any sooner."

Iris hesitates before going on. "That's a bright spot, that's good." She waits a second before she continues. "Let's get back to Mike from Hoboken. I know you're not going to take my advice. That's fine with me, but don't flirt with him to help lift your emotions from the blues you're feeling. I know you want to get out of the run of the mill life you're experiencing. You want to feel a little mysterious yourself. I feel that way sometimes, but I don't act on it, and neither should you."

Cass smiles, "Thank-you Doctor Iris. But I am going to the reunion. It's going to be platonic, that's all it's going to be."

"You are highly vulnerable to a romantic relationship right now. You have worries about Charles and you aren't getting the attention from him that you used to get. An admiring male can make matters worse. Don't let that happen."

"I'm not headed for any trouble. I'm mature and reasonable. If I felt seeing Mike would harm my marriage, I'd avoid meeting up with him."

"Then why were you so anxious to talk with me about Mike and your reunion?"

"Like I said, I think I'm just a little overwhelmed right now, but I feel much better now that I've talked with you."

"You're that sure you'd keep Mike locked up only in your fantasies?"

"Absolutely, positively sure."

Iris asks, "Have you told Charles that you've changed your mind about the reunion?"

"Not yet."

"When do you leave?"

"In two days."

"Don't you think time is running out?"

"I wanted to talk with you first."

"For what purpose, to try to convince you not to go, or to support your decision?"

Cass hesitates. "I'm not sure, but as I've said, I've made up my mind. I'm going."

Iris smiles, "All I can say is have a good time, but be careful. Don't let any sparks fly."

"You're a good friend, my best friend. Don't worry. It's just an innocent class reunion."

Iris is not convinced.

Ω Ω Ω Ω Ω

"Honey, I've got something to tell you." Since talking with Iris, Cass has recited over and over again the key points she intends to tell her husband.

"Yeah, what is it." Charles walks towards her. His three day old beard is scruffy and his hair is disheveled. His eyes are cast down. He is in the dumps.

"Remember about my class reunion?" She wishes her voice had some more oomph to it, but it is the best she can do right now.

Charles frowns. "Yeah, you said you weren't going."

"Well, I've changed my mind."

"Oh."

"I hope you're not upset."

"Why would I be upset?" He crosses his arms.

"I guess because I'd be leaving you and Scarlet Rose alone for a while."

"It's fine with me and I can't imagine our daughter would object."

"I'm relieved. I wouldn't want you to be worried."

"Worried about what?"

"I guess it's a wife-mother thing, you know, the homebody of the family."

"Nah, don't worry about it." His arms stay crossed.

"Did you get a call from someone who talked you into it?"

"Yes, that's exactly what happened." She tells herself it is not a lie. "I haven't seen these people for a long time, and well, I'm kind of curious to know what everyone's been up to. I wish you would reconsider going with me. It could be fun." She wonders if Charles picks up on her insincerity.

"Nope, you know how I feel about reunions. Anyway, I don't know anyone from your class. I'd be bored. You should go yourself."

"You're positive?"

Charles replies, "Maybe while you're gone, I'll find a job and everything will be back to normal."

"That would be great."

"I don't think I've been pleasant to be around these past few months."

Cass can't believe what she hears. She had expected a good deal of resistance from Charles and even a bit of resentment. She decides to tell a fib. "Oh, Charles, I know it's been stressful, but you haven't been unpleasant. I think you're handling the situation much better than I would under the conditions." She moves close to him, and puts her arms tightly around his body.

"Sure." He wonders about the sudden show of affection, but quickly puts the thought aside as nothing of importance, "When are you going?"

"In two days. You're sure you and Scarlet Rose will be OK?"

"Of course we will. Just have a good time."

Cass' voice sounds weak. "I'll tell you all about it when I return. I love you."

Ω Ω Ω Ω Ω

Cass steps inside The Grande Magnifica Albergo, looks around at the spacious lobby and spots the check-in counter. As she moves forward she hears her shoes click on the Italian marble floor.

A young man, black wavy hair combed back with teenage looks, smiles as she approaches. He has an Italian accent. "Good afternoon. Checking in?"

She spots his name badge. "Yes, Carlo, I am. The name is Cass Westfield."

Carlo drops his eyes to look at a computer screen to his right. He correctly types Cass' last name and within five seconds he looks up. "Signora Westfield. Sì, a reservation for two nights, one person, luxury room, no smoking, pre-paid."

Cass smiles his way without saying a word.

"May I have a credit card for incidentals?

"Yes, use this one."

Carlo finishes processing Cass' check in. "Here's your credit card and your room card for number 927. You also have a message." Along with the credit card and room card, he hands her a blue envelope embossed with **GMA**. He continues. "The elevators are to your left. Our lounge and restaurant are just past the elevators. Dinner begins at 6 pm. There is a 24-7 workout facility on the third floor that is amply equipped. Would you like assistance with your bag?"

Cass does not hear the rest of Carlo's comments. She stares at the blue envelope. Her face looks startled.

"Signora Westfield, is everything alright?"

She turns towards Carlo. "Uh, what?"

"I'm just wondering if you are alright. Is there anything I can do?"

"Oh, no, everything is fine. Thanks." She grips the envelope tightly in her hand. Where are the elevators?"

"To your left."

"Yes, thank you."

"Prego."

Cass grabs her bag and walks away a few steps. Then she stops. Unwilling to hold off until later, Cass opens the envelope. She reads,

Cass, it's been too long.
I'd love to have dinner with you tonight, my treat.
I'll call your room at six.
Mike

She feels her heart skip a beat. Emotions collide with each other as she tries to figure out what to do. She feels her face flush with excitement. On the way to the elevators she recalls the recent conversation with Iris about not acting on her emotions and to avoid temptations. She whispers to herself, "It's only going to be platonic."

Once she reaches the elevators, she presses **UP**. It takes a few seconds before the elevator door opens. She sees a man and woman about her age inside the elevator. Their arms hold each other tightly and their lips are firmly pressed against one other. Cass waits in silence to see what happens next.

The couple unlocks their grip on one another. They stroll out of the elevator holding hands as if nothing unusual happened.

Cass moves inside the elevator, presses **9**, and waits to let the elevator take over.

Ω Ω Ω Ω Ω

Once inside the guest room, Cass quickly walks to the bathroom. There she dampens a facecloth with cold water and pats her face. The impact of the cold water on her warm skin settles her down just enough to get on with unpacking. She checks her watch. It is a few minutes past five o'clock. Less than one hour to go before Mike calls. She feels her body reheat, so she commands herself, "Settle down. This is simply an innocent dinner with an old friend."

A knock on the door cuts short further self-instruction. "Yes, who is it?"

"Room service, I have a delivery for Signora Westfield." The voice has an Italian accent.

She is taken by surprise. "I'll be right there."

Cass slowly opens the door, nervous about what is on the other side.

A uniformed young man, spiked blonde hair and blue eyes, stands in the hallway. He bows slightly and smiles her way. "Signora Westfield, these are for you." He hands Cass a bouquet of red roses. He maintains a smile. "Enjoy your stay with us."

Cass is motionless for a short time. Then she reboots. As she takes the flowers, she notices his name badge. "Thank you Franco."

He slightly bows. "Prego." Franco starts to walk away, off to another delivery someplace in the hotel.

"Franco, please wait."

The young man turns to face Cass.

"Wait, I have something for you." Case moves towards a purse to find money.

He stands still.

"Here is something." She hands Franco three dollars.

"Grazie." He bows again, turns and walks away.

Cass slowly closes the door. Then she puts the flowers to her nose to take in the aroma. The perfumed smell settles her down. She spots a note card addressed to her. Slowly she opens the note to read,

Cass, you've always liked scarlet roses.
Mike

She reads the message again, and then tightens her lips. She places the flowers on a nearby table and then reaches for her cell. She dials Charles' number.

"Cass, what's up?"

"I just checked into the hotel and wanted to tell you that I arrived safely." Cass clears her throat, and then continues. "I love you very much."

"Yes, and I love you. Are you sure you're OK? You sound a little distressed."

"Everything is just fine. Just a good night's sleep and I'll be back to my old self."

"Great. Oh, by the way, Joe and Iris asked me over for dinner tonight."

"That's wonderful." She pauses. "What about Scarlet Rose?"

"She asked to be excused so she could study with a

few friends. I said it was OK as long as she and her friends studied at our home."

"She's a good kid, but she's growing up too fast. I'd rather she remain fifteen years old for a while." Cass hesitates again before continuing. "Anyway, tell Iris and Joe hello from me." Another hesitation and then she asks, "Is Scarlet Rose there? I'd like to say hi."

"No, she's with Wanda Parker at her house, but should be back here within the hour."

"Tell her I called and that I love her."

"I will. Now, get some rest. You sound like you might be coming down with a cold."

"Good advice. Good-bye. I love you."

"And I love you too."

The phone disconnects, yet Cass still holds onto her cell for a few seconds longer. Then she reorients her thoughts to finish unpacking. She does not notice the time has crept another fifteen minutes forward.

At five forty-five she finally sits on a king-sized bed, everything is put away. Then she notices the bouquet of roses still in a flat position on the table. She finds a nearby vase with artificial flowers, and replaces them with the scarlet roses. She adds just enough water to keep the flowers fresh. She checks her watch. It is nearly six o'clock. She would really like to rest for thirty minutes before Mike calls, but that is not in the cards. She lets her head drop back onto a pillow and then she closes her eyes.

The ring of the room's telephone at promptly at six o'clock startles her. Her body jumps a bit. Cass smacks her lips, and then reaches for the phone. She waits to hear who is on the line.

"Cass, is this you?"

The sound of the man's voice is familiar to her ears. The moment has arrived, and now it is her turn to reply. "Is this you, Mike?" She hears her voice quiver and wonders if it noticeable to him.

"It definitely is. I bet you haven't changed one bit, beautiful as ever."

She feels something deep inside awaken that has been asleep for some time. She gives no thought at the present time if she is headed for trouble. Her emotions are running the show. "Don't I wish. I bet you haven't changed either, as smooth and charming as ever." She flashes back to a time when she was flat-bellied, single, and drinking Pabst Blue Ribbon beer until early in the morning.

"There's only one way to find out. Are you ready?"

Cass feels as if she is the most beautiful and appealing girl in the world and he the most handsome and wittiest man around. "Can you give me a few minutes to freshen up?"

"Of course. How about having dinner here?"

"Sure, why not."

"Wonderful, I'll meet you at the entrance to the restaurant."

"Fifteen minutes at tops. And the roses are beautiful. You remembered my favorite after all these years." She feels giddy and radiant.

"How could I ever forget, you loved scarlet roses."

"You remembered."

"Yes I have. It's what you called them, scarlet roses."

"I'll see you in fifteen minutes."

"I can't wait to see you."

She figures it is best to cut off the flirtations before it

gets out of hand and the temptation too strong. She ends the conversation, "Bye."

As Cass changes clothes and freshens up she laughs to herself thinking about the times he shared funny stories with her when they were younger and unanchored.

Ω Ω Ω Ω Ω

She slowly steps off the elevator to make her way to the restaurant's entrance. She feels nervous and lightheaded at the same time as if this is a blind date. She stops after walking only a few feet, and turns to a large mirror nearby. She takes a final approving look at her appearance. With the brush of her hand she smoothes her white-on-white pinstriped silk blouse, and then realigns a thick grey belt around her waist. She steps back to glance at her black pants and pebble-grained shoes. Cass smiles at her looks. She moves towards the restaurant, and then spots Mike.

He is the first to speak. "You look as gorgeous as ever." He wears a white cotton shirt, three top buttons opened at the collar that uncover a hairless chest. His pants are midnight blue and his shoes are saddle double-monks. He extends his arms towards her as he steps forward.

Her face beams with happiness as she takes in the pleasure of seeing him after all these years. She willingly lets herself stay wrapped in his arms. The manly smell of his body brings back memories of the intimate times they spent together in college. Her eyes stay closed and her breathing settles into a comfortable rhythm. His magical charm continues its spell on her for a while longer. Then she slowly releases her embrace on him to let go. She pulls away with a certain amount of reluctance.

Cass' dreamy eyes slowly become alert. She takes in a deep breath of air. "You haven't changed at all since college."

His six feet frame stands motionless. His smile shows off his pearly white teeth, and his brown eyes appear intense with passion.

She continues to look at him, captivated by the spell he has over her. She is without words.

"I'm partial to someone like you."

Cass softly says, "And at one time I had a weakness for someone like you, and you've always had the right words to make me feel good."

"It's always been the truth."

Cass decides the teasing is close to getting out of control. "How about dinner. I haven't eaten anything since early this morning."

Unenthusiastically he says, "of course," but he'd rather do something else. He figures there is still the chance to have sex with her later on if he plays his cards right. "We'll start out with a PBR."

"I haven't had one since college."

"It seems only fitting."

He puts his arm around her waist and squeezes it just right as they walk into the restaurant.

She takes in the pleasure of his touch without any resistance.

A man dressed in a dark blue Canaletti suit, red and white striped shirt, and navy blue tie stands behind a stand. He smiles their way. He has an Italian accent. "Good evening. Do you have reservations?"

"Yes, two for 6 PM. The name is Aviara."

The maître d' looks down at the reservation book.

"Yes, I have something quiet and private. Please follow me."

During their conversations, Mike listens to Cass without interruption, offering at times a few things about himself.

Cass does most of the talking. "Well, after college, I went on to get my MBA with the plan of becoming a highly paid consultant. One thing led to another and I found myself working at an insurance company in the human resources field. My boss was great. He mentored me and gave me the right advice at the right time. Once he decided to retire, I was the most logical successor, but it didn't happen. The Board chose another person. So, I did the most logical thing I could think of at that time. I sent my résumé to headhunters and landed a pretty nice Human Resource executive job at another company. That's where I met my husband who was on a consulting assignment with them. We hit it off nicely, and we got married. He's lost his job since and is struggling to find something. It's tough out there, but he'll do OK. He's kind of depressed right now."

"With a wife like you, he's already a winner. He's a lucky man." Mike smiles warmly.

She blushes. "So, what's been going on with you?" Cass takes a sip of wine. One beer was enough, even if it was a PBR. It did not taste the way it used to when she was younger.

"I had to drop out of college to take care of family stuff, but eventually I finished on-line."

"Yeah, I always wondered why you didn't say goodbye."

"I had no choice. I'm sorry."

Her voice is suddenly sharp sounding, "Sure, no problem."

Mike picks up on the change in her tone. He knows why but lets it go for the time. He figures there is no use in bringing up past uncomfortable times.

Cass' voice returns to a less prickly sound. "What are you doing now?"

"I run the family business. It's a private company."

"And what is the business?"

"We offer a variety of consulting services to mostly small to medium sized companies. We specialize in safety and security." Mike smiles, but this time the grin is more serious than friendly.

"So, are you married, got kids?"

His voice is without emotion. "I lost my wife a few years back before we had a chance to have a family. So, I spend most of my time working. I travel a lot."

She does not pick up on Mike's matter-of-fact update. "Oh, I'm so sorry about your wife. What happened, or is this too personal?"

"I'd rather not talk about it. You know." He blinks a few times.

"I understand, sorry." Cass takes another sip of wine.

He changes the topic. "I still can't believe how fantastic you look. You're trim, your skin is smooth, you dress stylishly, and you're still a great conversationalist. What's your secret?"

Cass blushes, welcoming the compliment. She recovers, "You're not so bad yourself. How many hours a day do you put in at the gym and how do you keep your curly hair so black? Come on, tell me your secret and I'll tell you mine."

He enjoys the verbal exchange and now is more hopeful about having sex with her tonight. He eagerly ups the ante to increase the odds of that happening. "Do you remember that one winter Friday night when we hitched a ride from a police van?"

Cass laughs as she remembers the event. "And we didn't know they could hear everything we said because there were microphones and speakers in the back of the van that recorded everything!"

Mike leans toward Cass as if to whisper something private. "I remember each time we made love and where."

Cass' eyes open wide, surprised. She hesitates momentarily to encourage the line of conversation. She knows this is a forbidden temptation. But then she gets into it, to do one up on him as if they are in a contest of memories. "You must have a great memory because there were many-many times." She leans back in the chair, flickers her eyebrows, and juts her chin out to challenge him further.

Mike picks up the contest. "Which one was best for you?"

"Oh, come on." She quickly backs off from the contest, realizes she should avoid this type of challenge.

"No, really, I bet you don't remember any of them." Mike is prepared to a face-off with her.

"This is silly. Those situations happened such a long time ago."

Mike's alluring smile compels her to continue.

Cass frowns for a few seconds, and then says,

"OK." Then she pauses to reconsider whether to take the conversation further. Her emotions take over. "I remember one time when we were swimming in the lake, near campus." Her eyes gleam with excitement as if she is experiencing the same condition now. "No, I can't go on, this is foolish."

Without any hesitation, he says, "No it isn't." His captivating smile is front and center. "I remember that time, just like you do." He waits for her response.

Cass blushes.

"If you're not going to tell the whole story, then I will."

"No, Mike, let's not do this." She shakes her head sideways. She pats her lips with a cloth napkin.

"You're blushing." He grins at the sight of her embarrassment.

She pulls herself together. "That was a real long time ago. Things are different now. Let's talk about something different."

He lifts his shoulders. "It was a while back, but isn't it remarkable how we both remember them so clearly, as if it just happened." Then he smiles.

Cass senses they are entering a dangerous zone when their thoughts could become action. She decides it is best to get out of the situation. She checks her watch. "It's late and I'm getting tired. Travel does that to me. I think I need to call it a night." She puts the cloth napkin on the table.

Mike does not give up. He leans across the table and starts to sing. His voice is faintly heard. "Well, I'm hot blooded, check it and see. I got a fever of a hundred and three. Come on baby, do you do more than dance? I'm hot blooded, I'm hot blooded." He pauses for a second and then says. "Remember Foreigner, and the song we used to sing when we danced?"

A slight smile slowly creases her face. She twists her nose to the side and then begins to sing in a voice that is barely heard. "If it feels alright, maybe you can stay all night. Shall I leave you my key?" Cass suddenly stops. She shakes her head sideways. "No, that was way too long ago." She pushes her chair away from the table. "I really have to go."

"A guy can dream."

Cass stands. "And I really need to head back to my room. I'll see you at the reunion dinner tomorrow night."

Mike is pushy. "No sooner?"

She heaves a sigh of uncertainty but quickly refocuses, "Mike, we were together a long time ago when we were single and carefree. Now is different."

"Let me at least walk you back to your room. I'm just enjoying being with you so much." He looks seductively into her eyes. "Nothing more, I promise."

She is not convinced.

Ω Ω Ω Ω Ω

As Mike steps inside the elevator, he asks "What Floor?"

"Nine." Her voice is calm for the moment.

Mike presses the button and the elevator doors slowly close.

Cass leans against the cold wooden elevator wall. Her heart beat suddenly quickens. She keeps her head down focused on the brown tile squares lining the elevator floor praying that Mike cannot see her hands shaking. She swallows just enough to get some saliva down her throat.

"It's really great to see you again, after all this time." His eyes look fondly at her. His smile is wide and bright.

At Mike's comments, Cass looks up to find him staring intently at her. She is unable to hide her emotion. Her face brightens.

He slowly moves so close to her that she feels her cheeks redden.

"You are so beautiful, Cass."

Her cheeks flush again.

"Especially when you blush," Mike adds.

She never was good at accepting a simple compliment.

Mike continues to stare at her intently. He moves a hand across her cheek, and gently tucks a piece of loose hair behind her ear.

His touch sends a shiver through her and she instinctively turns her body towards him. Her mouth opens slightly as if to say something, but words are not necessary.

Mike reaches for her hand and pulls her even closer. He puts his hand on her face once again, slowly outlining her cheek, then her jaw and slightly grazes her bottom lip with his thumb.

She feels her entire body's nerves react to his touch as she is not able to remain motionless. She wants to give herself entirely to him right now.

"I want you, Cass." Mike whispers softly in her ear, and gently kisses her cheek.

Cass does not think of turning away, as her body stays prepared for his next move.

Mike's kiss moves from her cheek to her jaw. He pauses and looks into her eyes. Before she can react, he pulls her waist into him and kisses her hard on the mouth.

The shiver runs through her body again and her face is hot.

His lips are soft and yet strong as they press against hers. Mike shifts Cass' waist away from him and against the wall.

She enjoys the weight of him against her body and feels herself wanting more. She lets out a soft moan as she feels him grab her hand tight against the wall and kiss her passionately.

As Cass' heart pounds, Mike moves his hand to the most sensitive spot on her body, centered and just below her waist.

She lets out another soft moan, this time more inviting for him to continue. "Yes," she whispers. Cass thrusts her pelvis towards Mike. "Yes," she repeats.

His hand gently massages her. "I want you, Cass, more than ever."

She moves her face close to his and kisses him hard on the lips. With her back now against the elevator wall, Cass feels the cold wood against the small of her back. She enjoys being pinned, being the subject of his compassion, taking in whatever he gives her and then more.

Mike kisses her neck and moves his hand back to her waist, caressing her lower back. His hand travels to where her shirt rests lightly on top of her pants. His fingers touch the skin on her waist and hips. With his other hand, he grabs her hand.

More electric shocks run through her body and she knows she will not resist him. "Go on."

The elevator beeps loudly, announcing their arrival on floor nine. At this interruption, Cass pulls her face away from Mike.

He lets go of her waist, but does not release her hand. He leads her out of the elevator and into the hallway.

Cass feels the heat slowly leave her face, but her body still shakes, not over with his presence.

They walk together speechlessly until they reach her door.

"I should go to bed," Cass says as she reaches for her room key. Even to her the words are not convincing.

Mike smiles and there is a wicked gleam in his eyes. He pulls her hand to his chest and places his other hand on her cheek. He always knew exactly how to render her speechless. He leans in to kiss her again exploring her mouth with his tongue and gently biting her bottom lip.

Cass feels Mike reach for the key card in her left hand and lets him take it from her.

He pulls away from her to open the door.

Cass hesitates for a moment, but allows herself to be led into the hotel room. The room is dark and smells of the scarlet roses delivered just a few hours earlier.

Mike pulls her into the center of the room. He traces his hand from her neck to her shoulders.

Cass shutters.

"I want to make love with you, Cass," Mike whispers once more in her ear.

Cass closes her eyes and feels her breathing speed up again as it did in the elevator.

Mike places his hand on her back, kisses her hard,

and leans her back towards the bed. His hands search her body in the right places. As he lifts her blouse up he sees Cass instinctively arch her back. Mike lifts her top over her head.

Cass looks into Mike's dark eyes and hears his quick breaths.

He kisses her neck and she can feel his hot breath on her sensitive skin. His hands move over her collar bone to her breasts.

She feels her nipples harden under his touch and her hands grip his back tightly in response. She feels his hands reaching to unbutton her pants and she helps kick them off. Her head feels dizzy.

Mike pulls away from her to remove his shirt, pants and shoes.

She takes a moment and looks around the dark room. There on the desk her eyes rest on the scarlet roses.

Ω Ω Ω Ω

"This was a great idea. You're both good friends." Charles leans back in his chair, takes another sip of wine. "But I think I should go home."

Joe tries to change his mind. "No, it's still early. Cass is at her reunion and Scarlet Rose is safely at home. You'll just flip on the television and have another drink by yourself. Stay just a little longer."

Iris chimes in, "Yeah, Charles, just one more glass of wine and then we'll all call it a night."

"OK, just one more." Charles finishes off the remaining wine in his glass.

"I'll get another bottle while the two of you boys sit tight." Iris leaves them alone for a while.

Silence slices through for a short time.

Joe asks, "How is the job search going?"

Charles answers. "I'm not getting any job leads from my job search. It's really frustrating, and to be honest, humbling to be living off of Cass' salary. I mean, I know she's making good money and all, but, you know, I think it's pride that's bothering me."

Joe's face turns somber. "Have you thought about going back to school or learning a new skill set? I mean, the work scene is changing so rapidly, it's hard to keep up with what's current and what's not."

Charles shakes his head sideways. "I think one degree is enough. I'm not interested in getting another one. And about new skills, I wouldn't know what new skills to learn. Like you said, everything is changing so quickly, what's in today is out tomorrow. No, I'm stuck where I am."

"You're still a relatively young man. You don't want to get into a rut of repeating the same stuff over and over again. Habits are powerful and you don't want to get into bad habits."

Another head shake from Charles, "Yeah, but it's not easy."

"As an attorney I've got to take courses just to keep my license. That's the way it is."

Charles pauses. He is thinking of something different but isn't sure how to say it. Then he blurts out what is really on his mind. "I wouldn't know what I'd do if I lost Cass."

Joe's eyes open wide, surprised at the change in conversation. "What do you mean? Is she ill?"

"No, her health is fine."

"Then what is it, is there some trouble between you two?"

"A little strain between us since I lost my job. I'm not my usual self."

"I don't know what that means."

Charles twists his face. "I'm crabby."

"Is that it, nothing more?"

"I'm not sure." Charles blows out a puff of air. "It's about her class reunion. At first she wasn't going to attend and then all of a sudden she decided to attend. I'm not about to complain about her having a good time, but I haven't seen her so keyed up in a while."

"Are you suspicious of something?

"You sound like you're interrogating me."

"You know I'm an attorney. That's just how we talk. I'm sorry, I should tone it down."

"See what I mean? I'm all worked up and can't think straight."

"Maybe you're jealous that she's having a good time and you're not."

"Maybe so."

"Why didn't you go along? I'm sure she would have liked that?"

"She asked me, but I said no. I'm just not interested in that sort of thing. I've never attended any of my class reunions so why would I attend one where there's no one I know? It just doesn't make sense to me."

Joe cocks his head to the side. "Maybe to do it for her and her alone, not for you and not for any other reason."

"Really, you think so?"

"All I'm saying is that sometimes, as husbands, we

need to do things for our wives to please them in spite of the fact that it displeases us. It keeps marriages going. I think sometimes people our age get too comfortable in relationships, we take them for granted. I know you love Cass deeply and she loves you, but sometimes we have to show it in much more obvious ways. That's all I'm saying."

Charles listens without saying a word, yet his mind is thinking over a few things.

"Saying you love Cass is OK, but showing that you love her is better."

Charles remains quiet.

Joe continues. "I love Iris so much that I wouldn't know what to do if we weren't together. I guess the fear of losing her keeps me motivated to make sure our relationship is working out. I really don't like attending art galleries, but she does, so I agree to go with her. Sometimes, I even suggest a new opening she's never heard of. She knows I love sports so she joins me in watching games on television, even though I know she doesn't particularly care for sports. It's just how it is. It's our way of keeping each other."

Charles asks, "Have you ever suspected that Iris might have close male friends?"

Joe frowns, and then figures out the real meaning of the question. "If you mean in an intimate way, then no." He pauses and then continues. "Are you suspicious that Cass has something going on with someone?"

"I really don't know."

"Then why did you bring it up?"

"I don't know, really, I don't know."

Iris overhears their conversation from the kitchen. She wonders what Cass may be up to.

Ω Ω Ω Ω Ω

The next morning Cass is the first to wake. She sees Mike sleeping soundly alongside her and immediately realizes what she's done. She feels the beginning of a panic attack. She says to herself, "I've just had an affair." She quietly gets out of bed to walk to the bathroom.

She stares at a reflection in the mirror, yet the image is someone she does not fully recognize at first. "Why did I do this?" She rubs her face in hope of clearing up the likeness of someone she knows. "What have I done?" She thought she'd feel like she did when she was in college, young and pretty. That, however, is not the case. She feels tired and ugly, someone who has betrayed her marriage commitment.

Cass returns to the bed where Mike still lays sleeping. She bends over to shake him. "Wake up, it's time for you to go." Her voice needs a little more oomph to be convincing, so she gives it a second go. "Hey, wake up! You've got to leave right now!"

Mike turns over to face Cass. A smile slowly spreads across his face. "Good morning. You were wonderful. Come here, let me hold you." He extends his arms.

"No, get up and get out! I should never have done this! It's over! Please leave now!"

Her voice does not persuade Mike. He does not even flinch at her words. "I know you don't mean it." Mike sits up in bed.

Suddenly a buzzing sound interrupts their conversation.

They each look at a nearby cell phone.

Cass reaches for her cell to notice Caller ID. "Hi honey," she says cautiously. She points to Mike to go to the bathroom.

Mike slowly gets out of bed and purposely takes his time to move away.

"I just thought I'd call to see how everything is. I miss you. I wish I had decided to come with you."

Cass' eyes begin to water. "That's so sweet. I miss you, too. Tonight's the reunion dinner."

"What did you do last night?"

No matter how happy and innocent she tries to sound, she is convinced it is not working out as she hoped. "Uh, I had dinner with a few friends at the hotel. It was good to see them."

"That's great to hear."

She clears her throat. "How was dinner with Iris and Joe?"

"Wonderful. I wish you were there." Charles feels his throat slightly constrict.

"That's so sweet." It is all Cass can think of saying. She is not fully listening to what Charles is saying.

"Well, I'll let you go. I just wanted to tell you how much I love you. I can't wait for you to be home."

"I love you too, I really do."

The cell disconnects.

"Can I come back?"

"Yeah, you can come back now."

Mike strolls back to face her, "I guess that was your husband."

"No kidding." She is displeased with how things are going but convinced to make it right. "It's time for you to go. We're not going to see each other again under any conditions. I don't want to lose my marriage. So, it's time for you to go, right now."

"Do you really mean it? Come on, no matter how happily married you are, isn't there room for a nice man like me who wishes you were not?"

"Mike, let's be serious. This is too dangerous for me. I simply won't have it. Now, please go."

Cass realizes that her words are much different than the unspoken attraction she feels towards him. She would really like to have it both ways but she is determined to leave him in her memories and fantasies, like having a memento in her pocket that only she knows exists.

"I think you're making a big mistake, but I won't argue with you." Mike puts on his clothes and leaves without saying another word. He knows deep down they are not through with each other. In fact, he intends to make sure of that.

Ω Ω Ω Ω Ω

Now alone, with nerves almost shredded to pieces, Cass sits in a nearby chair to settle down. She is uncertain how to handle the matter. Then, she glances around the hotel room to spot the flowers from Mike propped up in the vase. Her lips tighten. She quickly moves off the chair toward the roses, pulls them out of their vessel, and tosses them into a nearby trash can. If her stare were only more violent looking, the flowers would wilt away.

"This ends it for good."

Ω Ω Ω Ω Ω

Mike's face is angry. He is accustomed to getting whatever he wants, and is not pleased with Cass' decision to boot him out of her life. He does not believe her display of will is strong enough to overcome his desires. He has no intention of going away.

Outside The Grande Magnifica Albergo, Mike makes a call on his cell phone to one of his wise guys, Lou D'Amico. "Find out everything you can about Charles Westfield and his wife Cassandra. I don't want to wait long for the information."

CHAPTER 2

Later the same day Cass readies herself for the class reunion dinner. She nervously paces her hotel room. Her mind switches back and forth on whether to go through with it. She is still shaken from what happened last night and this morning with Mike. "Just put it out of your mind. What happened then won't happen again." She nods her head to further convince herself of the resolution, yet something deep inside her fights off a full commitment. "I know he's going to show up at the dinner, so I have to act neutral toward him. I have to!" She hears her own deep breathing and then stands still for a moment. Her eyes drift towards the hotel room's telephone. An idea pops into her head. She reaches for her own cell phone.

After two rings, she hears his voice. "Hello?"

"Honey, it's me." She wonders if Charles hears the quiver in voice. She tries to settle down.

"Hi, what's up?" There is a tinge of surprise in his voice.

"Oh, not much, just putting on the final touches for tonight's dinner."

"Oh, I see. How's it going so far?"

"Well, I should have taken your advice."

"What was that?"

"Earlier this morning I said that seeing old friends last night was great, but to be honest, it was all so boring. I don't know what I was thinking when I said that. I almost decided not to attend tonight's dinner. I'm not sure what I'll have in common with anyone. You were so right on."

"Since you're already there, just try to enjoy it. You might bump into someone special."

Cass delays with a response. "I miss you."

Charles continues to listen.

"At least if you were here we'd both be down in the dumps." She sniffles just a bit. "I'll be home tomorrow. There's no sense staying here any longer than my original plans." Another pause before she continues. "How are you doing?"

Charles hesitates before he explains to her what he has decided. "I've figured that I've got to change my ways. I thought about what you said earlier, you know, about staying up to date with my skills."

"That's wonderful. I'm so proud of you."

"Next is the tough part."

"What's that?"

"You're going to have to help me figure out what I can do."

She wipes away a few tears from her eyes. "We're in this together. You can count on me."

"I've always known that. You've been my rock. I don't know what I would do if you weren't by my side."

Cass holds off with all her might a loud cry. She manages to say, "I love you so much, I'll do anything for you." She wants to ask him to forgive her for all the lies, but she holds back.

"And the same from me. I'm going to be a changed man when you come home. I promise."

Silence cuts through their conversation.

Charles manages to pick up the talk. "Don't you have to get going? I don't want you to be late."

Cass replies. "Yes, you're right. There's a reception of some sorts before dinner. I'll see you tomorrow. I love you."

"I love you, too."

Ω Ω Ω Ω Ω

Cass enters a large room set up with a cash bar and a wide assortment of hors d'oeuvres. She stops to survey the place. She figures there are at least one hundred people mingling around. At first she does not recognize anyone. She strokes her black silk dress at the sides, takes in a deep breath, and steps forward. She thought she would feel all choked up with delight at this exact moment, but right now she is ill at ease. The unnerving emotion quickly changes when she recognizes a voice call out to her.

"Cass Horizon! Is this really you?" A short woman awkwardly walks closer. She is overweight, dressed in old-fashioned clothes, and with a hair style that is outdated. Her puffy face looks tired. "I'm so happy you changed your mind."

Cass looks towards the voice. At first she does not recognize the woman who knows her by her maiden name. Then her recollection becomes clear. "Leslie Merrill!

Amazing, you look the same as when we were in college." She decides a tiny lie is in order.

"Yeah, just like I was in college, except for about twenty pounds heavier and more wrinkles than I care to admit. But thanks for the nice words. You're the one who looks terrific. How do you manage to stay so trim and attractive?"

"Now who's piling it on?" Cass smiles brightly.

"No, really, you look terrific."

Cass feels more comfortable now than just a few moments ago. "OK, I'll accept the compliment." She turns her body once around. "What have you been up to?"

"I'm married to a great guy, Tom Balsom. We have two wonderful sons, Bob and Pete. I volunteer at the school that my boys attend, and Tom is a procurement manager. Typical average family. What about you?"

Cass clears her throat. "I too am happily married to Charles Westfield who, unfortunately, is in-between jobs. I have one fifteen year old girl, Scarlet Rose."

"Oh, what a pretty name."

"Yes, thanks." She feels a tickle in her throat. "She's a wonderful daughter."

"Is your husband with you? Tom couldn't make it."

"Same with me, I'm solo."

"You'll never guess who RSVP'd." Leslie's eyes widen with excitement.

"I have no idea. Who?"

"Mike Aviara. You remember Mike, don't you?" She waits for a response that does not come. Then she adds, "You should remember him."

The unpleasant feeling Cass felt just a few minutes ago returns tenfold. She takes a hard swallow to calm down. "Oh, Mike Aviara." She pauses with a deep breath of air. "I sort of remember him. That was such a long time ago."

"Sort of! Unless you are losing it completely, you and he were real tight throughout college. Everyone thought you and Mike would settle down together, have kids and live happily ever after."

The tickle in her throat returns. "Really?" She coughs and then goes on, "I'm surprised to hear that."

Leslie shrugs her shoulders. "Anyway, he RSVP'd. I'm interested to see what he looks like. He was sure a head-turner at that time." She steps closer to Cass. With a whisper she asks, "I wonder if he is still mixed up with the Mafia?"

"The Mafia, come on, that was a rumor that had no merit. But to be honest, I really don't know. After college we didn't stay in touch. I don't know what ever happened to him. In fact, I'd forgotten about him until you brought up his name."

"Maybe one of us should ask him?" Leslie flickers her eyebrows.

"I really don't care one way or another."

"Anyway, do you remember Jean Breg?" Leslie decides to change the topic.

"Sure do. She was probably the most attractive girl we knew. Everyone thought she'd become a famous Hollywood star. Why are you asking?"

"Well, don't say that it came from me, but she's had a rough time, really rough." Leslie touches her lips with her index finger.

"I'm sorry to hear that." Cass is not interested in hearing about other people's problems for the moment.

She figures she has a few of her own that need to be dealt with.

"See the woman by the bar who's wearing a short black mini dress with a red belt, and long black hair?" Leslie nods her head in the direction of the cash bar.

Cass angles her eyes in the direction of a group of people near the bar. "Yes. She's talking with a few men who seem quite awestruck with her."

"She's had multiple marriages and as many divorces, can't seem to keep a man for any period of time, mostly older men. That's Jean Berg." She wiggles her eyebrows. "But I'm told she isn't financially hurting. Evidently, she's had favorable premarital arrangements with her fiancés that have worked to her benefit. She must be pretty convincing or have a good lawyer."

Cass isn't interested in the subject, so she keeps her answer short "Maybe both."

Ω Ω Ω Ω Ω

At the corner of her eye, Leslie spots someone walk into the room. Her eyes light up as bright as a Christmas tree ornament. She slowly paces the words. "Get … a hold … of him!"

Cass turns in the same direction to spot Mike Aviara. She closes her eyes and begs to go unnoticed. However, she does not keep them shut for long. She sees him staring directly at her.

"That's Mike Aviara! He looks more handsome than he did in college." Leslie does not take her eyes off of him. She waves her hand to get his attention. "He's coming our way."

Mike is dressed in a dark blue Tendenza fashioned suit, white shirt and red tie. His black curly hair is neatly cropped. He confidentially takes long strides towards the two women. While he does not recognize Leslie, he makes out Cass. A smile titivates his face with pearly white teeth that take center stage.

Leslie whispers to Cass, "I feel all excited inside, if I faint, you'll have to catch me."

Cass is not grateful for the turn of events. She begins to formulate a plan to quickly distance herself from him. She wants to make a run for it before he arrives.

Before Mike has a chance to say anything, Leslie makes the first move. "Hi Mike. I'm Leslie Merrill Balsom. I'm so glad you could make the reunion."

Mike's broad big smile captivates Leslie, but leaves Cass feeling uneasy. "Of course I recognize you. How have you been?"

Leslie almost giggles. She feels young and unencumbered for a short time. "I'm doing well." It's the only response she can come up with at the moment.

Mike carefully keeps his eyes glued to Leslie, and away from Cass for the time being.

"I'm sure you two remember each other." She nods towards Cass. "This is Cass Horizon Westfield."

"Of course, Cass. How could I ever forget? It is so good to see you again after all these years."

Cass manages to say, "Hi Mike."

Mike asks, "Are you here alone or with your husbands, lovers, spouses, significant others or whatever the politically proper phrase is these days?"

Leslie is the first to answer. "My husband couldn't make the reunion. I'm, well, on my own tonight."

An uncontrolled flicker of her eyebrows sends off an involuntary flirty message.

Mike picks up on the flirt but ignores it. "I see." He turns to Cass, "And you?"

"Same as Leslie."

"What about you Mike? Alone or with someone?" Leslie is eager to find out.

Mike ignores her question. "Leslie, what do you do?"

Leslie is eager to please him. "I'm one of those stay-at-home moms. I've got two great boys, Bob and Pete. I volunteer at the school my boys attend. Tom is a procurement manager."

Mike turns to Cass, "And you?"

Cass forces a weak smile. "I have a good job in Human Resources. Charles is currently in-between jobs. I have one teenage girl." She is not interested in sharing anything more than what she's already told him earlier.

It is Leslie's turn to get into the conversation. She returns to her original question. "Mike, what do you do?"

Mike ignores the question from Leslie again to turn towards Cass. "If Charles is interested in making a career change, maybe I can help him. I know several companies looking for good people."

Cass feels awkward talking about her husband knowing she's just has an affair with Mike. "Thanks for the offer but he's got several opportunities in the hopper right now."

Leslie says, "What a nice offer. Thanks Mike." She is persistent to return to her previous question.

Mike, what do you do? Are you married, got kids, you know the usual stuff?"

"I run the family business. We specialize in security systems for small to mid-sized companies. I travel a lot. Been married but she died before we could have any children. So it seems all I do now is work."

"Oh, I'm sorry." Leslie says. There is an awkward silence before Leslie asks another question, "There's no reserved seating at the tables. What do you say we all sit together?"

"Fine with me," Mike quickly answers.

"That will work fine," Cass halfheartedly says. She figures there is no way to get out of the situation.

"Can I buy you ladies a drink before dinner?" Mike offers.

"I never pass up a free drink. Gin and tonic," eagerly replies Leslie.

Mike looks at Cass who remains quiet. "And you, what will you have, PBR?"

Cass clenches her teeth. She does not want to give in to the temptation of enjoying herself with him, especially in front of Leslie. It is over! "I haven't had that beer in ages. No, I'll have a glass of chardonnay."

"Don't go anyplace, ladies. I'll be right back." Mike turns to leave Leslie and Cass.

Ω Ω Ω Ω Ω

"I'd go anyplace with that man. He's absolutely gorgeous!" Leslie stares at Mike as he walks away. "Look at that tight ass. I wonder what exercises he uses."

"You'd be willing to spoil your marriage over him?"

Leslie flickers her eyebrows. "I'd keep it hidden from Tom."

"I don't believe you. It's just your imagination running wild." Cass steadies her eyes on Mike as he self-assuredly walks towards the bar.

Leslie angles her head towards Cass. "You mean to tell me if you and he could have one night together without anyone knowing about it, you'd say no?"

"I'm saying no, and so should you."

"No matter how happily married I am, it would be wonderful to know that another man wants me."

"It's not worth it."

"I can't believe you've never thought about having an affair with another man." Leslie frowns. "In your job you probably have men both younger and older than you giving you flirty looks."

"Whether or not that happens, and I'm not admitting one way or another, I wouldn't jeopardize my marriage, definitely not, no way."

"Cass, I don't believe you. In fact, it might bring the marriage even closer."

"Leslie, that's the wildest rationale ever made. Don't fool yourself. It's just too dangerous, and hell, it's against the marriage vows. Come on, get serious."

"I disagree. I'd jump on the opportunity if Mike was interested in me," Leslie admits.

Cass shakes her head sideways. "Let's agree to disagree but we should drop the topic. He's coming back with our drinks."

Leslie admiringly stares at Mike as he gets closer.

"Here are your drinks, just as ordered. Let's toast to

forever friendships." Mike raises a bottle of PBR high in the air.

"Yes, to friendships," Leslie takes a sip of her gin and tonic.

"To friends," Cass chimes in with some timidity.

"I recognized a classmate, Barb Evans who is with her husband Ryan. Talking with Barb and Ryan was another classmate, Jake Kelpie, whom I had not met before since tonight. I invited them to join us for dinner. I hope that's OK with you. It'll be great to catch up with them."

Leslie replies first. "Terrific. I haven't seen Barb since college. I don't remember Ryan and I don't know Jake."

Cass remains quiet.

"Is it OK with you, Cass?" Leslie asks.

"Oh, yeah, sure. I was just thinking about Charles and wished he was here, too."

Mike ignores Cass' lament and says, "Great. Would you look for an empty table of six and lift the chairs against the table to reserve it while I tell them we're fine with the arrangement?"

Leslie answers, "Cass and I'll do the real work." She gives Mike a big smile who returns one of his own. "Come on, Cass, let's get on with it."

Mike separates from the two women.

Ω Ω Ω Ω Ω

The dining room is large with twenty circular tables, six chairs to each table. Most of the chairs are occupied. The table cloths are white and there is a large garnet and grey banner on one wall identifying the college name and logo. Waiters busily start the process of serving the same appetizer to each person; a ginger fruit cocktail composed of freshly sliced banana, fresh halved strawberries, melon balls, and sliced apple parts that had been marinated in ginger ale and lemon juice.

"Do you all remember each other?" Mike asks to allow everyone to greet each other.

Barb starts it off. "Hi, I'm Barb Evans Thompson and this is my husband Ryan. As you can see, I'm expecting. This will be our third child." She pats her stomach and fondly looks at Ryan to kiss him on the lips.

"Like Barb said, I'm her husband. I've never met any of you before since I was in the School of Humanities. But I did meet Barb at a basketball game when we were seniors. All it took was one look and I was forever captured." He affectionately looks her way.

"I'm Jake Kelpie. I'm here alone. I was real quiet in college and I don't think I've met any of you before either." He is a large man, well over six feet four inches tall and easily two hundred pounds of muscle. His friendly looking face and soft spoken voice further adds to his charm.

Leslie says, "This is wonderful, isn't it. I mean, we haven't seen each other since those carefree college days. I'm Leslie Merrill Balsom. I remember Barb, Cass and Mike, but yeah Ryan and Jake, this is the first time we've met."

Ryan is silent and Jake blushes.

Everyone turns to Cass. "Hi, I'm Cass Horizon Westfield and like Leslie I remember her, Barb, and Mike. Sorry Jake and Ryan, I don't think we ever met before tonight."

Jake drops his eyes in embarrassment. His face blushes with a deeper shade of red. He hears his stomach growl.

He wonders if anyone else heard the same noise but he is too self-conscious to look up.

Leslie looks at the appetizer. "This looks great, bon appetite."

Ω Ω Ω Ω Ω

Dinner is almost over, along with the consumption of several bottles of wine. Everyone sits quietly for a short time, not sure how to end the evening, or if it should conclude at all.

Barb is unable to hold back a yawn that is noticed by everyone. "I'm so sorry, nothing to do with the company. I get tired easily." She smiles as she looks down at her stomach.

"Yeah, me too." Ryan smiles at his wife. "With two young ones at home and another along the way, we don't get out much. I guess we're both out of practice for this sort of thing." He leans over to kiss Barb on the lips.

Cass wishes Charles was by her side, to give him a big kiss and hug. For a moment, her mind freezes with that thought in place.

Barb and Ryan stand to leave together. They hold hands.

Leslie is not eager to end the evening so soon. "While I'm out of practice as well, I'm ready to get back into shape." Her eyes scan the remaining others around the table.

While Mike is interested in something else, he asks Cass, "How about you, Cass, care to join Leslie and me for another drink at the bar?" He ignores Jake who sits quietly.

Cass shifts out of the self-imposed thought of her husband. "I'm not sure. I've got an early flight tomorrow."

"Oh, come on, just one drink before you go. We're probably not going to see each other for a while after tonight, maybe never again." Leslie is excited about the idea of extending the evening to as long as possible.

Cass takes in a deep breath, head tilts towards the table without looking at anyone, and then she glances towards Jake. "I'll have one drink, only one, if Jake comes along."

Jake is surprised by the acknowledgement. He shakes his head, no. "I'm not much of a night owl. Up early and back in bed early. I think I'll call it quits." He stands. "I've really enjoyed this evening. I wish everyone happiness." He starts to walk away.

Cass interrupts, "Oh, come on Jake. Just one drink. I'd like to know more about what you've been up to these days. You've been the quietest of us." She thinks she has camouflaged the real intent of the invitation. She is worried what might happen if she and Mike were left together.

"I know I'm shy and well …" Jake does not finish the sentence. He really wants to call it a night, but feels pressure building against him to change his mind.

"Oh, come on, Jake," Leslie joins in. She figures that if Cass and Jake get to talking with one another, she has more of a chance to be with Mike.

Mike quickly picks up on what is happening, and he does not like it a bit. "If the guy wants to be left alone, we should let him be. Come on, don't pressure Jake." He has already settled on a plan to be alone with Cass and does not want anything or anyone to interfere.

Silence wedges through the conversation for a short time.

Mike gives Jake an evil eye that goes unnoticed.

Cass glances at Leslie, gives her a slight grin. Then she angles her head towards Jake as she touches his arm. "Come on, one drink."

Jake feels his face redden and his body heat up. Confused at first as to what to do, his next impulse seals the deal. "Alright, just one drink." He turns towards Cass to help pull her chair away from the table.

"What are you two waiting for? Let's go." Cass thinks she has shaped the evening's plan, but she has no idea what Mike is capable of doing.

Ω Ω Ω Ω Ω

The lighting in the hotel's lounge is dim. Jake catches sight of a booth. "There's a spot in the corner. OK?"

"Show us the way," Cass says.

Jake leads them to the place. He steps aside to let Cass slide in, and then he follows. Leslie and Mike sit across the table. "This is nice," Leslie says.

A nearby waitress notices them, and comes over to take their drink orders. "Hi, what can I get you?"

Leslie orders first, "Gin and tonic."

Everyone looks at Cass. "Your house Chardonnay will be fine."

"I'll have a rum and coke," says Jake.

"What, no one wants a PBR?" Mike looks around to

find him alone in the choice. "I'll have a PBR and Haig Scotch."

"Got it, be right back." Once finished the waitress leaves them alone for a while.

Cass notices Mike's face is covered with disappointment. She concludes he does not approve the seating arrangement. She smiles to herself in satisfaction.

Before Cass can ask Jake a question, Leslie beats her to the punch with a question to Mike. She turns to Mike. Her voice is slurred and uneven from too many drinks. "There's been somethin' … I've always wanted … to ask you in … college … but never did."

Mike frowns, wonders where she is headed. He shrugs his shoulders.

Cass and Jake look on, surprised. They both pick up on Leslie's inebriation. Jake is eager to hear more while Cass thinks she knows where Leslie is going.

"In college … there was this guy … he was real big … you know… who followed you around … as if he was a bodyguard … or something. Several of us wondered … wondered … what that was about … you know … but no one ever had the guts to ask you. What was … what was… that about?"

Mike realizes Leslie has had too much to drink. He wants to ignore her comment but instead he flashes back to those times when his father controlled his every move, something he hated and would have done anything to end.

Mike decides to put it all out, so he says in a matter-of-fact way, "He was a bodyguard."

"Oh … oh," Leslie says.

Mike clenches his teeth as he tries to beat down his

temper. Then he slowly wills himself to relax. "I hated the bodyguard watch my every move more than anyone could ever imagine, but there was nothing I could do about it. Several times I tried to pay off the guy, but that only got me into more trouble when he snitched me out."

"Wow!" Jake says.

Cass decides to enter the conversation. "Why was there a bodyguard?"

Mike goes on. "There were lots of idle gossip and news reports that implied my family was Mafia related. Yet, in all the investigations and scrutiny there was never one piece of evidence to prove any link to organized crime. The idea that my family had connections and alliances to unsavory people hung over them. Even today, as much as I try to dispute it, people are suspicions of me. People think I'm connected to the mob. Isn't that a piece of crap?"

"So, your parents just wanted to make sure you stayed out of trouble, did your work, kept your nose clean, is that it?" Jake asks.

"That's about it. No more to report." Mike says. He glances around to the others. He grins.

Jake adds, "I never thought you were part of the mob. Never gave it a thought."

"And you Cass, what did you think?" Mike's eyes roam her face as if he is inspecting a piece of property he intends to buy. He is not able to hold back a slight smirk.

The waitress arrives in the nick of time. "Here are your drinks." After she places each drink on the table, she sets a bowl of pretzels in the middle. "Anything else I can get you?"

"No, we're fine," Mike snaps back as he continues staring at Cass.

She jerks back at Mike's roughness. "No problem. Give me a holler if you want something." She leaves the foursome to pick up again where they left off.

Mike presses Cass to reply to his earlier question. "And what did you think?"

Cass takes a sip of her drink, and then coldly says, "Never gave it a thought." Slowly she lifts her shoulders up and slowly resets them.

Jake gives the conversation between Mike and Cass no particular importance. "Like I said I never gave it a thought either."

Leslie is quiet as she awkwardly takes a sip of the gin and tonic. A few drops of liquid dribble down her chin.

Thirty minutes pass slowly and it is a little agonizing to everyone. While the idea to get up to speed on each other's lives seemed good at first, it is not turning out that way now.

"I think it's time for me to go. I really enjoyed being with all of you." Jake extends his hand towards Mike. "Take care." Then he looks at Leslie and Cass. "It was great." He slides out of the booth, stands and is about to walk away.

"I think I'll go, too. I've got an early flight." Cass skims her body along the wooden booth to stand alongside of Jake. "I'm glad I came to the reunion."

"No, we've got more to talk about." Mike sounds as if he is shouting an order. Wrinkles appear on his forehead.

"Not for me, I'm headed off." Jake is impervious to the interpersonal dynamics.

Cass grins towards Mike. "Sorry about that." She takes Jake's arm, "Let's go."

Mike and Leslie watch Jake and Cass walk away together.

Leslies takes a deep swallow of her drink. Without looking at Mike she says, "She … deserved it." Her words continue to be slightly indistinct from one too many drinks.

Mike continues looking intently at Cass. "What?"

Leslie turns to face Mike. She slowly pauses between each word. "I … said … she … deserved … the … rough … treatment … from … you."

Mike glances towards Leslie, "You mean Cass?"

"Who … else?"

"I wasn't rough with her."

"That's … just … my … opinion. Take … it … for … what … it's … worth."

"You're drunk."

Leslie ignores the accurate observation and begins to fantasize. A smile spreads across her face, while her head is tilted downward.

Out of the corner of his eye, he gets a glimpse of Leslie. "It's not going to happen." Mike looks straight ahead at the spot where Cass sat. "Not going to happen, so don't waste your time thinking about it."

She temporarily sobers up but her words run together. "What do you mean?"

"Listen, Leslie, I'm not stupid and I'm pretty good at reading body language. I've got nothing you want. Go back to your family. They're the ones who love you."

She slaps him on the face. Her words continue to be slurred. However this time she speaks rapidly. "Don't be so conceited. You don't know me and never did. In college all you wanted was to be with her, and you were. But now, things are different. You can't have her and you are fuming. Now, get out of my way so I can get as far away from you as possible. I never want to see you or hear from you ever again. Now, move."

Slowly Mike slides away from the booth. He keeps quiet.

Leslie looks directly into his eyes. "You are disgusting and foul." She stumbles out of the booth, a little tipsy, and manages to hurry away that leaves him standing alone.

Mike gets back into the booth. His head nods a few times. He has made up his mind about something. Then, he waves to the waitress to order another drink. He reaches for a few pretzels that he efficiently gnashes with his teeth. He whispers with firm determination, "She belongs to me."

Twenty minutes later Mike leaves the bar. He walks a few feet and suddenly stops.

He notices Jake and Cass sitting in opposite chairs in the lobby. She leans toward Jake in what appears to be a serious conversation. Jake seems to be listening in earnest.

Although he cannot make out what they are talking about, just the same, Mike feels a mixture of jealously and anger. He feels his temper start to heat up. He wants to put an end, once and for all, to the situation. He steps back out of sight to think things over and to continue watching them.

A few more minutes pass before Mike sees Cass and Jake stand. She puts her arms around Jake and then kisses him on the cheek. Then she says something to Jake that

Mike cannot hear, but seems to please Jake as he nods his head in agreement. Jake extends his hand to shake with hers, and then she walks away. Jake looks on as she soon disappears around a corner towards the elevators.

Jake turns to walk outside towards the parking garage. He spots his SUV just up ahead and pulls out his car keys. Then he hears a familiar sounding voice yell out. He turns around to spot Mike facing him.

"Hey, you, I want to talk with you." Mike is slightly hunched over, shoulders somewhat turned in, and fists clenched tightly.

"Yeah, what's up?"

"I saw you and Cass together. I don't want you to ever talk with her again. Do I make myself clear?" Mike's voice is angry sounding and menacing.

"What?" Jake is confused.

"You heard me. Stay away from her or else."

"What are you talking about?"

"Let me make this as clear as I can so that even a bozo like you can understand. She's not yours, will never be yours, so stay away from Cass. Is that clear enough?"

"What are you talking about?"

"I saw the two of you make your secret plans to get together. She's mine, all mine. If I ever see the two of you together I'll put an end to it, permanently. She belongs to me!"

"Are you threatening me?" Jake steps closer now realizing what is going on.

Mike pulls out a gun. "I guess you got my message. I'll put you down with one shot to your head."

Jake steps back, and raises his hands. "I understand. I'm going. Don't shoot."

"Yeah, now get out of here before my finger gets itchy."

Jake turns and hurries away.

Mike watches Jake disappear into his SUV, and then he returns to the hotel. He has unfinished business.

Ω Ω Ω Ω Ω

Mike knocks on the door to guest room 927. "Cass, it's me. Please let me in. I want to apologize for tonight."

The sound of Mike's voice startles her. She is not expecting him and indeed wants him to stay away. She pauses for a few seconds as if to decide what to do. While her instincts tell her to be quiet, to ignore him, she is hesitant. She hears another knock, and figures he is not giving up.

"Cass, I know you're in there. This will only take a minute or two to apologize. Then I'll go, I promise."

She closes her eyes to maintain the courage to disregard the awaiting temptation. Part of her does not want to be pulled towards him. She knows what will probably happen if they come together. She whispers to herself, "Stay calm and be quiet, he'll go away."

A third knock on the door settles it all.

Underneath an ankle-length white-cotton robe Cass only wears panties. She slowly walks towards the sound, turns open the locking mechanism, and opens the door. She stands motionless, face to face before Mike. Then she softly says, "No, this won't work." With her left hand she grabs hold of the robe near her throat to clench it tight. She shakes her head sideways and steps back, away from him. Her voice is weak and unconvincing to her but it is the best resistance she can muster.

However, his seductive smile controls the situation. He steps inside her room without using force, and then he closes the door. Other than the clicking sound of the door's lock, there is silence.

Cass offers no struggle. There is no need to talk. She knows why he has turned up.

As Mike lifts her into his arms to carry her to the nearby bed she wraps her legs around his waist and her arms around his neck until he gently rests her body on the king-size bed's cotton quilt cover.

She lets her legs and arms relax as her head softy touches the bed's pillow. The robe unwraps at her waist to reveal her smooth legs. Her eyes remain open, and her breathing is even and effortless. She parts her lips to say something but only a moan is heard, and then it fades away.

Still standing, Mike looks deeply into her eyes. Then he slides alongside her and brushes his hands, gently and purposeful, underneath the robe and against her breasts. He squeezes them with care.

She feels her nipples rise underneath his large hands and makes no effort to resist his progress. A satisfied smile covers her face.

As Mike moves one hand between her legs her nerves come alive, touched in the right spot and in just the right way. A whispering sound of contentment makes its way to her lips. "Ohhh, Mike."

He gently massages her, senses her pelvis rise to get into rhythm. He repositions his hand to slide between her soft skin and undergarment. His finger finds its way into a warm and moist opening. He tenderly glides it in a circular fashion and smiles as she arcs her back in deliriousness. Still on her back he reaches with his other hand to pull away her underpants.

Cass spreads her legs wider for him. She knows what is about to happen and welcomes it. At first she feels his face, and then his lips, and finally his tongue. She is unable to remain still, her hips move, first slowly and then quicker. The sound of his tongue touching her moist skin causes her to lose rhythm. She lets out a silent yell. She feels hot and wet all over and for an instant does not know where she is. She doesn't care; she wants the feeling to last longer and to be more intense. Minutes pass before the ecstatic sensation ends, only a slight tingle remains. She unlocks her eyes. Her vision is a little blurry.

Mike slips off his shoes and then takes off his shirt, pants, and briefs. He bends over to slide his hands along the curves of her body. "Stay still." He speaks softly. "You're beautiful."

Cass smiles, lets him do what he wants and what she craves. Then her eyes lower. "Let's change positions. I want to be on top."

He repositions his body to look up at Cass.

She reaches for him, holds and then gently squeezes him until he is stiffened. She opens her mouth and then moves her tongue across her lips. "It's my turn," she whispers.

He remains still for a split second, and then his eyes widen. His skin begins to feel warm. He shuts his eyes in order to feel the fullness of her strokes, and then her mouth and tongue wrapped around him.

She keeps him drawn into her mouth making a sound similar to a baby taking milk from its mother's breasts.

He grabs her head with both hands all the while mentally transported to some other place.

Minutes later Cass frees her mouth and coquettishly asks, "You've got something for me?" She does not wait for his answer as she guides him into her. She feels her hips move without willing them. She grabs his face, hungry for him, and presses her mouth against his.

Now in full penetration, Mike begins to thrust, confident in knowing what he is doing. He feels the warmth of her body, both of them moving together, first slowly and then more quickly.

She clings to him, calls out his name, and then feels him go off inside her. Instantly, she explodes.

Their bodies collapse into each other's arms. They stay embraced for a short time not wanting to say anything or needing any conversation. They lay side by side until both fall to sleep.

Outside Cass' room, Leslie walks towards the closed door. She flattens her ear to the door to listen in. She says aloud, "I'll … be." She slowly shakes her head sideways, and then walks away. Aloud she says, "What a … phony … she is."

Ω Ω Ω Ω Ω

The next morning Cass wakes up before Mike. She blows out a breath of air, looks at him still soundly sleeping, and then slowly gets out of bed.

She walks towards the bathroom, closes the door, and gives a long stare at her reflection in the mirror. "What am

I doing? I've been over him for a long time. I'm married. I have a daughter. What the hell am I doing?" She turns on the basin's faucet and messily splashes some water on her face. Then she refocuses on the mirror's image. "This is it. I'm going to tell him it's over, and this time I mean it." She nods her head once to reinforce the pledge. "I give my word it's over."

After toweling her face dry she returns to the bed where Mike remains asleep. Cass bends over and slightly nudges him. "Hey, wake up. It's time for you to go."

"Ah," Mike turns his body away from her. He is still asleep.

Cass takes in a deep breath and gives it another try. "Hey Mike, get up!" With greater assertion she presses against his arm. "Come on, it's time for you to go!"

Slowly Mike turns her way. He is now awake. His eyes open slightly at first, and then wider. He yawns and arches his back. "Come here beside me." He stretches his arms to beckon her closer.

Cass raises both hands upward, "No more. It's time for you to go. Now get up, please, and leave."

Mike frowns, turns his head slightly to the side. "What? Go? We've just got reacquainted."

"It's time to end this. It is time. You've got to go. We can never see each other again."

He sits up in bed. "You can't be serious."

"Oh yes I am, very serious."

"What happened? I thought we were getting along fine, just like we used to."

Cass shakes her head. "That was then, and this is now. I'm married and have a daughter that I don't want to jeopardize. I think it's pretty simple to understand."

"I understand."

"I don't think you do or else you'd leave."

Mike rubs his face with both hands. "You simply don't tell them. See, I do understand, it's that simple."

"You've got to be kidding me?"

"No, I'm serious. Just don't tell them. I won't."

Cass shakes her head sideways, "That's simply ridiculous, what kind of person do you think I am?"

"I think you still want to be with me, just as I want to be with you."

Cass says, "At one time but not now. I've changed. Obviously you haven't."

Mike looks off to the side. "I started out as a good kid."

Surprised by the change of topic, Cass asks, "Where are you going with this?"

"I was a good kid, really, but something happened to me."

Cass frowns. "You went over that earlier this evening. I get it. Your father was a control freak, just like you've become."

"But you don't know the whole story."

"And let me guess, you want to tell me now."

"Yes I do."

She crosses her arms and keeps quiet.

"In my senior year, I was told he was dying."

Cass puts her hands to her mouth. "I'm so sorry."

"I rushed to see him ... you know ... before he died, but I was too late."

"So you never had the chance to say goodbye to your father? You must have been distraught."

"Well sort of."

Cass asks, "What do you mean, sort of? Didn't he die before you could say goodbye?"

"I was so angry that I didn't see him suffer before he died! I could have cared less about saying goodbye! As far as I was concerned it was good riddance to get him out of my life!"

Cass remains motionless and quiet. She feels slightly confused.

"I hated him."

Cass keeps quiet as she moves to a nearby chair. She hears herself breath in and out.

"I took over the business and have made something of it. But, I'm surrounded by loneliness, so I need someone to love and be loved. You're the obvious one. He didn't care about me then, and my mother, where ever she is, doesn't care either."

Cass manages to say, "I was devastated when you took off without even saying goodbye. You disappeared from me and I never heard from you for all those years, not even a call."

"But now you have, I've returned." He smiles. "And we can be back together again."

She shakes her head sideways. "I wish it was that easy. It's much too late for that." She straightens her back. "I'm sorry for what you've been through, but it's time for you to go, and, you can never contact me again."

"You're still angry and hurt after all these years, even after I've told you what I've been through? I'd take back whatever suffering I caused you in an instant if I could. All of it."

"I swore that if I ever saw you again, I would smack you in the face for what you did to me. Now I'm a little settled down. But you don't know how many times I thought I saw you nearby, yet it was only my imagination. I thought you'd come to me, but you didn't. Then, along came Charles. He gave me what I needed most."

"And what was that?" Mike asks.

"He gave me self-confidence. I felt attractive, desirable, worthy and a good person. He made me feel like someone he wanted to be with for his entire life. He made me feel needed."

"But you were always attractive and desirable to me and many other men. You must know that."

"That's only part of it. Haven't you heard what I said?"

His voice is sarcastic sounding. "Evidently not." He has about had enough of the talk.

Cass is not through. She has more to say. "But a woman not only likes to be told that, to be reminded of it, she likes to be treated that way. That's just how it is."

"And Charles is the one for you, is that what you're saying?"

Cass takes in a deep breath. "Yes I am. Further, he is my place of safety. He would never leave me. He'd stick by me whatever I did. He's that loyal and committed to our marriage."

"Even if he knew about us?"

Cass' eyes widen with anger. "You wouldn't!"

Mike smirks without replying.

Cass repeats. "Don't you dare!"

Mike keeps silent as he shrugs his shoulders.

"Then I guess I'll have to tell him everything. I know he'll understand."

"Really, you'd tell him?"

"Yes, that's right."

"And you're positive he'd understand that you've have a sexual affair with an old boyfriend. Come on, be serious. He'd throw you out of his life at the drop of a dime."

"No, not Charles. He loves me unconditionally. I'm one hundred percent positive."

"Too bad you can't say that about yourself."

Cass raises her voice. "Get out now or else I'll call security! Go!"

CHAPTER 3

A full week passes since the reunion. Cass' return to a normal life style with Charles after the class reunion is dull and boring, not what she had hoped for and what her husband had promised. She wonders if she should give it more time. One week may not be sufficient. She longs for something, or perhaps more appropriately, someone, to spice up her life. Mike is the obvious first one to come to mind, but she hesitates, not sure she would be able to control her emotions if they were together again. She continues to be baffled by the lure of Mike, the temptation he represents, and her uncontrollable urge to be with him. She knows it's wrong, but she can't find the strength to stop it. She figures the best approach for a distraction is to stay busy. But long hours at the office and neurotic physical exercising can do just so much.

It is the wee hours of May 27th, a Thursday, and Cass tosses and turns in bed. The repeated nightmare she's had over the past several days of falling from the sky lurks notably in her psyche. She stares at the white ceiling, not sure what else to do at the moment. Her temples throb a bit, the result of sleep deprivation and one two many glasses of Chardonnay before going to bed. She unsuccessfully commands herself back to sleep. Frustrated she perches her body upright, looks to her right, and is startled. Charles is absent. She calls out, "Charles, are you here?"

Silence is the only response, so she makes a second effort, "Charles, where are you?" The reaction is the same as before, so she slowly lifts the bed sheet off her body. Now standing, she slips on a robe and walks towards the bathroom. She calls out again, "Charles, where are you!" Her voice is now louder and sounds distressed. No one answers.

A nearby clock indicates 1:20 am. Now wide awake, she wonders if her husband is sleepwalking again or if he somehow found out about her indiscretions and decided to leave her. "There is no way he knows about Mike and me," she whispers softly. Yet down deep inside she wonders what she would do if the tables were turned. She moves to other rooms upstairs. The result is the same.

Finally, she heads for Scarlet Rose's room to peek in. Her daughter is soundly sleeping. Cass smiles at the one who represents the bright spot in her life. She softy says, "I love you."

Next she heads down the stairs and moves toward the kitchen. She calls out again, "Charles, where are you?" but as before there is silence. Out of the corner of her eye, she notices the kitchen sliding backdoor is ajar. A worried frown takes center stage on her face. She steps forward to take a look.

To her right is a light switch. She flicks it on to illuminate the backyard. At first glance, the backyard seems normal. Red roses are in bloom, the grass is green, and water sprinkles from the automatic watering system are evident. She breathes in the early morning's fresh air. It feels refreshing. She is about to turn off the light when she notices something unusual. Slowly, she slides open the screen door to step outside. At a snail's pace she cautiously moves one step at a time. Then she sees him.

Charles is curled up on the ground like a child, soundly sleeping as if without a care in the world. His pajamas are intact but damp. He is barefooted and his hair is ruffled.

Cass remains stock-still. First, she covers her mouth with both hands for a second, and then for some reason she looks around. No one else is around, but then she notices the backyard gate is open. She rushes to Charles. Now alongside him she kneels. The nature of the dampened parts of his nightclothes is clear. The color is red and she realizes it is blood. She reacts, "Oh my God!"

Cass is frantic as she places her hands on his arms. "Charles, Charles," she says as she gives him a shake. However his body does not respond. She tries again, this time with more force, and calls out his name louder, "Charles, Charles!" This time she gets a reaction.

"Ah." The sound is faint yet audible.

Her hands continue to rest on his arms. "Charles, it's me, Cass, your wife, what happened?" Her hands are now partially smeared with blood.

His eyes slowly open. He smacks his lips together in an attempt to get some saliva flowing inside his mouth. "Ah." His voice is only a bit stronger.

"Are you hurt?"

"Where am I?"

"You're with me, Cass, your wife. Are you hurt?" She

sees a confused man in front of her, and now she is even more frightened than before.

Charles shakes his head sideways, and then he uncurls his body. "What happened?" He takes in a deep breath of air.

"You don't remember?"

"Where am I?"

"You're in the backyard with me."

He sits upright, looks around, and then notices the blood on his clothes. An alarmed expression covers his face. "What's this?"

"Blood, I'm sure of it." She stares a while and then continues. "You really don't know what happened?"

Charles ignores the question. "Blood, how did that happen?" He asks, confused still.

"I don't know." She takes in a deep breath of air and then puffs it out quickly. "Are you hurt? Did you fall down? Do you know what happened?"

"I have no memory of this." Charles looks frantically at Cass.

"First things first, let's get you back inside and cleaned up." Cass stands. "Here, take my hand."

He grabs her hand firmly and slowly stands alongside her. He is a bit wobbly so he takes hold of her shoulder with the other hand. "I don't know what happened."

They move to the kitchen.

"Here, sit down in this chair while I get something to clean up your skin."

Without a comment, he does as he is told. His head tilts downward as he places his hands on the kitchen table.

Her mind is now fully functioning. She can only

conjecture what happened. "I think you were sleepwalking again, and you fell." Cass pauses. "Maybe it was something else, I don't know."

He looks up at her. He is terrified. "I don't remember anything."

She sits down beside him and then gently washes blood off of his arms. "This will hurt just a little," Cass says as she dabs scratches on his skin with liquid antiseptic. "Stay still."

Charles squirms, "Ouch."

"I said it might hurt. Don't move your arms."

He starts to think more clearly. "I'm afraid."

"You've been so good for such a long time, and then it started again. I wonder if something triggered it. What do you think?" Cass continues cleaning Charles' skin. She is thankful that he is willing to talk about it, something she had previously believed would never happen.

Charles continues to be lucid. "I bet it's my employment status. Cass, it's really taking its toll on me."

"I know, I wish I could help, I feel so powerless."

"It's not your fault, it's mine."

"But I am a Human Resources professional. I should be able to get you connected for at least informational interviews, something, anything that might help you network."

"It is what it is." He glances between Cass and his arms. "I've got to find something to do or else I'll go crazy. I need to get connected to someone who has some pull. That's how people find jobs these days. They network, but I'm not real good at it."

The shift of topic should help reduce their anxieties but all it does is shift it from one topic to another.

Then she remembers during the reunion reception Mike's offer to help Charles with a career change. She clearly recalls Mike saying he knew several companies looking for good people. Maybe he could talk with a few people to get Charles connected? But as quickly as that idea comes to her she shakes off the thought. She has to forget about him forever. It is much too risky. She continues cleaning his arm.

"I'm running out of lies telling Scarlet Rose why I'm around the house so much. If she hasn't done it by now, she's soon going to put a few things together." Charles shakes his head. "Ouch, that hurt."

"Then don't move your arm so much." Cass continues to clean the scratches. "And don't be such a baby." She gently pats his skin. "She is fifteen and old enough to understand that people get laid off from work. We should tell her the truth. It's always better to tell the truth in spite of how much it might hurt."

"Honey, I'm not ready to be hurt that much. I mean … it's taken her a while to accept me as her father. I don't want to disappoint her any further," Charles says.

"She loves you as her father. She doesn't remember her biological father when he died. She was too young. It's you who is not prepared for the truth. I think it's about time you get over it." Cass finishes cleaning his skin. "It looks like scratch marks from a cat or a dog. I think we should report it to the police."

"Please, no." His eyes plead her to agree. "Please."

Ω Ω Ω Ω Ω

Later on the same day, a frantic woman dials 911. "Someone killed Taffy!"

It is not unusual to receive 911-emergency calls that are misleading or completely false. Those who receive 911-emergency calls are trained to stay calm and ask critical questions in order to determine the level of triage.

"Please tell me your full name and your home address?"

"Taffy is dead! Someone killed her!"

"Please tell me your full name and your home address."

She sniffles. "I-I'm Margaret Yule. I live at 2761 Edgewood Avenue."

"Yes, thank you. Who is Taffy and what happened?"

"I don't know what happened! Taffy is dead! I found her in my backyard this morning. This is dreadful. I don't know what I am going to do without my Taffy!"

"Who is Taffy?"

"She's my best friend. I don't know what I'm going to do without her. I'm all alone now."

"Can you describe Taffy?"

"She's small, black and white, cute, and very well behaved. Her eyes are so beautiful, dark brown."

"So, Taffy is not a person?"

"That's right, but she often acts like a person, but not anymore. Taffy is a terrier."

"I see. How do you know someone killed her?"

The woman begins to cry but manages to say in between sobs, "Someone had to. Her small body is all mangled."

"I see. I'm going to transfer your call. Don't hang up. Do you understand?"

"Yes, I do. My poor Taffy, who would want to do this to her? She never hurt anyone, she loved everyone and everyone loved her."

Ω Ω Ω Ω Ω

It is late Saturday morning, several hours after finding Charles in the backyard. Charles and Cass sit across from each other at the kitchen table. The bottle of antiseptic and blood stained cloth are put away.

"I'm not calling the police and I don't want you to. This will all work out once I get a job. I just know it." Charles takes another sip of coffee. "I just know it will all work out."

"I hope you're right and I hope no one is hurt. I don't know what I'd do with myself if I found out someone got hurt." Cass stares off for a short moment at no place in particular.

"Like you said earlier this morning, you thought the scratches looked as if they came from a cat or dog. No one got hurt. I got scratched from a cat or dog, and I probably got the worse of it." He grins at the last remark.

"Just the same, I hope whatever it was that you tangled with is OK."

Charles decides to change the subject. "Did I tell you I got a call the other day from one of your college friends, Mike Aviara?" He sets the cup on the table.

She frowns, surprised with the news. "What, you got a call from whom?"

"I guess it slipped my mind. I think it was just a courtesy call to make me feel better, nothing of much importance."

"Mike Aviara?" She feels her throat constrict so she swallows deeply.

"Yeah, he said he went to college with you and saw you at the reunion. At first I was sort of surprised he wanted to talk with me, not you. He seemed like a nice guy on the phone."

Cass feels her stomach knot up, so she takes a deep breath to settle down. "Oh, yeah, Mike, I think I sat at the same table with him along with a few others. What did he want to talk with you about?"

"You won't believe it, but it was nice of him just the same to give me a call."

She commands herself to settle down. "So, tell me." She wonders if he hears her voice quiver as much as she does.

Charles stands to refill his coffee cup. "Want more? I can make another pot if you want more."

"No, no, I'm fine. But I'm curious about what Mike wanted to talk with you about."

Charles refills the cup, pushes a button on the coffee machine to shut it down. He lingers for a while as he takes another sip of coffee. "Well, he said you mentioned to him about my situation." He returns to take his seat at the kitchen table.

"The job situation?" She feels her body tighten.

"Yeah, what other situation could there be?"

"You're right, nothing else." She begins to feel a little relieved for the moment.

"You didn't say anything about my sleepwalking, did you?" His eyes widen a little.

"Of course not, why would I do that?"

"I don't know, I guess I'm still keyed up from earlier this morning." He looks at his scratched arms.

"I-I must have said something about your job search, but honestly, I don't remember. It might have been just a passing thought."

"You must have made a good impression on him."

"Maybe, I don't know. Anyway, I really wasn't into the reunion as much as I thought I would be. You were so right from the gecko. It turned out to be dull and boring." She feels her heart beat pick up a bit again.

"I see. Well, anyway, he said he knew people who might help me find a job. I guess the guy is connected somehow."

"That was awfully nice of him." She wonders to herself what Mike's real motive is.

"I'm not taking it very seriously. I think it was just a pep-up call to boost my self-confidence."

"Yeah, I guess so."

"Everybody needs a pick-me-up."

"Yeah, I guess so."

"What does he do?"

"He didn't tell you?"

"Not that I remember, and I don't think I asked."

"I think he said he runs his family business but I never asked him specifically what that meant. I mean ... I really wasn't much interested."

"Mike said he'd make a few calls on my behalf and get back to me in a few days." He takes another sip of coffee. "It's real nice of him to do that, right out of the blue, even it was just encouragement." Charles pauses.

"Yeah, I'm surprised as well."

"As I said, I'm not counting on it leading to anything, but it's hard not to get my hopes up."

"I'd be interested to see where it goes."

"He said he might have to take a business trip soon that would take him close by. I told him to give me the details so we could have him over for dinner. You know, as a thank-you."

Cass feels her throat tighten as air passes with some difficulty. She feels a little dizzy of the thought of being with Mike and her husband at the same time.

"What's the matter, your face has gone red?" Charles sets the coffee cup on the table.

"Oh, you know, one of those flashes women get, nothing to worry about."

Ω Ω Ω Ω Ω

"Hey." Scarlet Rose's soft voice calls out to her parents. "What's up?" She walks into the kitchen and heads for the refrigerator to pour a glass of orange juice and take a container of yogurt.

Charles answers, "Hi sweetie."

"What are you two talking about? I sense I've interrupted some adult stuff." Scarlet Rose smiles, kisses her mother on the cheek and takes a seat alongside her parents. Then she kisses her father on the cheek. "Not talking, huh."

"Nothing very important anyway," Cass says with little conviction.

Scarlet Rose glances at her father's arms. "What happened to you?" Her forehead wrinkles a bit.

He glances at his scratched arms. As casual as he can, he says, "Oh, this?"

"Yeah, looks like scratches from a cat."

"Actually, it's from trimming the rose bushes in the back yard." He is proud to have quickly thought of the answer.

"Ever think about wearing a long sleeve shirt?"

Cass decides to jump into the conversation. "See honey, that's exactly what I've been saying." She forces a smile to calm herself down.

He shrugs his shoulders.

Scarlet Rose says, "Duh."

"Next time, I promise," he says with an apology as strong as he can muster up.

Scarlet Rose scoops out a spoon of yogurt from the container. She hesitates as she lifts the spoon to her mouth. Unworried, she says, "I know all about it." She opens her mouth to take-in the food.

Charles frowns, looks at Cass who replicates the action, and asks, "About what? What do you know about?"

"I know how hard it must be to get a job." Scarlet Rose's voice is matter of fact. "A couple of my friends' dads are out of work, too. I know. I wish I could help."

"But there's nothing to worry about. We're going to get through it." Cass puts the best spin she knows how.

"Oh, I know. I'm not worried." Scarlet Rose takes a sip of orange juice. Then she turns to face her father to give him a kiss on the cheek.

"We love you," Cass softly says.

"And always will," Charles adds.

Poised with self-assurance beyond her age of fifteen years, Scarlet Rose calmly says, "I know." Then she takes another sip of orange juice before taking another spoonful of yogurt.

A nearby cell phone interrupts the conversation. "That's mine, I'll get it." Charles steps away from the kitchen table. "Hello?"

Cass continues to stare in admiration of her daughter as Scarlet Rose finishes off the yogurt.

"Hey Mike. How's it going?" Charles listens for a short time before he continues. "That's wonderful news. Thanks so much for doing this. And yes, Tuesday is fine. Do you want to talk with Cass?" He listens a bit more before continuing. "No bother, she's right here." He listens again with another pause. "Sure, I understand. You know how to find us?" Charles takes another pause. "That's the right address. We'll see you Tuesday evening around seven. Thanks again." Charles disconnects the phone. His face beams with pleasure.

Cass asks, "What was that about?"

"That was Mike Aviara."

Cass' eyes widen with further unease. An alarm bell goes off in her mind. "What did he say?"

"He's arranged a job interview for me with an executive search firm. Can you believe it?"

"Who's Mike Aviara?" Scarlet Rose asks.

Cass ignores her daughter's question. "An interview? With whom and for what kind of job?"

"Bent and Brooks is the name of the executive search firm. Mike said they'd tell me more."

Scarlet Rose repeats her question, "So, who's Mike Aviara?"

Again Cass ignores her daughter. "I've heard of the executive search firm, but I've never worked with them.

But, Mike doesn't even know what your skills are or what kind of work you've done before. I can't imagine him getting you an interview under these conditions."

"Hey, babe, it's an interview just the same. I'm lucky enough to get one, so I'm not going to worry about the details. If it doesn't work out then I'm right back where I started. At least it's a step forward."

"Hello?" Scarlet Rose asks again, this time with a bit of annoyance. "Who's Mike Aviara?"

Charles looks at his daughter. "He's a college friend of your mother."

"Oh, an old boyfriend?" Scarlet Rose wiggles her eyebrows.

Cass frowns, "No, nothing like that. Just someone I knew a long time ago."

Charles adds, "And he was one of the people she met at her class reunion. He's helping your dad find a job."

"Did you ask him to help dad?" Scarlet Rose asks as she looks at her mother.

"Not exactly, no." Cass' feels her throat constrict again.

"Then why would he help? I don't get it." Scarlet Rose tilts her head slightly to the side. "But it's real nice of him to do that."

"Sometimes people just do good things to help someone else out. I think that's all there is to this," Charles answers.

Cass knows there is more to it than an act of kindness. Her antenna is up. She has reason to be suspicious. "What was that about for this Tuesday evening?"

"Oh, when we first talked I asked him over for dinner

if he'd be in the area. I want to meet this guy." Charles says harmlessly. "I hope that's OK."

"Me too. Is he good looking, mom?" Scarlet Rose asks naively.

Cass clears her throat. "You know what they say about beauty."

"Yeah, in the eyes of the beholder. But do you think he's good looking?" Scarlet Rose asks again.

Cass feels her body heat up a little. "I don't know, maybe." She clears her throat and then moves close to Charles. "But not nearly as handsome as my husband." She puts her arms tightly around him.

"Good answer," Scarlet Rose says with a big smile. She joins her parents in a group hug. "I can't wait to meet him."

Cass feels her body tighten, and then she slowly pulls away. "Ah, meeting him might not be a good idea."

Scarlet Rose asks, "Why?"

The simple one-word question is sufficient.

Charles frowns and asks the same question, "Why don't you think she should meet him? He's helping our family and I think she should meet as many good people as she can."

"Um, I-I think the conversation at dinner will be more adult oriented. She'll get bored quickly." Cass realizes the comeback is weak.

"I may be only fifteen, but you've always said I act more than my age. I don't think I'll be bored. It'll be fun." Scarlet Rose's face is sincere looking.

"Won't you have homework to do? It is a school day." Cass tries again, but doubts if she is persuasive enough.

"I'll make sure I finish everything before dinner. I

promise. Cross my heart." Scarlet Rose moves her index finger over her heart to emphasize the promise.

"I think it'll be OK, really I do." Charles adds. "If she gets bored then she can always excuse herself."

Cass sighs deeply. "OK, I guess it'll be alright."

"Let's hug again to seal the deal," Scarlet Rose says with a good degree of poise.

Ω Ω Ω Ω Ω

The next few days pass slowly for Charles but much too fast for Cass. He wants to get on with the job interview whereas Cass is not keen on dinner with her family and Mike.

Late Tuesday morning Charles puts in a call to Cass. He is excited and speaks fast. "Honey, it went well. The executive search firm passed me onto the company and I think they liked me."

"Slow down. Who is the company and what is the job?"

Charles clears his throat and then proceeds in a slower pace. "First Floor Solar. They're a relatively new solar energy company who has funding to last about three years. They're looking for someone with good business savvy to be their chief administrator. You know, someone who's good at general management, paperwork, and keeping the processing stuff running well. I can do that, I've done it before." He feels his heart pick up and soon feels out of breadth.

"That's amazing. I've never heard of them before, but again, that's not my industry. I'm so happy for you."

"Yes, it is amazing. And to think that it all came from

Mike, your college friend. I'm glad I didn't convince you to skip the reunion. This would never have happened." His breathing quickens.

"Ah, did you get a job offer?"

"No, they said they have to check a few references before the job offer. But it sounded to me as more of a formality than anything else. I should be getting a follow up call later this week."

Cass' thoughts turn to something less positive. She begins to wonder how the evening will turn out.

OK, we'll talk more about this tonight."

"I love you." Charles says. "If you were here beside me now I'd undress you and make love like you've never experienced it before. I feel so alive."

Cass is surprised by the unexpected show of affection. She is jubilant with the idea. "Oh, Charles, I wish I didn't have a luncheon meeting scheduled. Damn."

"Can you get home early for a …"

Cass quickly interrupts, "Quickie?"

Charles answers with a smirk on his face, "You've read my mind."

"Stay primed until five."

"I'll pick up the things on the list you gave me and get everything ready for tonight's dinner. I wouldn't want to cheat into our time together."

"I'm feeling warm all over just thinking about it. Now, go, but save up your energy for me."

"I hope you'll live through the experience. There's going to be more." Charles proudly grins with passion.

Ω Ω Ω Ω Ω

Cass lays flat on the bed, face up. Her eyes are still swirling from the outburst of expression from Charles. She smacks her lips and takes in a deep swallow of air. Softly she manages to ask, "Where did this come from?"

Charles is positioned similarly along side. His face beams. He is proud. "I love you so much. I know I've ignored you over the past months. I'm sorry. It will never … I mean never … happen again."

"If it takes a little ignoring to get what I just got, then disregard me on occasion." She smiles.

"I'll never turn my back on you." He closes his eyes to emphasize the commitment.

Silence slices their conversation for a short time.

Charles takes in a deep breath. "Will you do me a favor?" A little grin appears at the corners of his mouth.

"Anything, just name it." Cass frowns, not sure what he means.

"One more time before dinner. Huh?"

Cass grins and then positions her body on top of him. "If you get it up, I'll ride it."

Ω Ω Ω Ω Ω

The front door bell of the Westfield residence rings at 7 PM. Scarlet Rose runs towards the door to be the first to greet Mike. She opens the door and immediately extends her hand to shake. "Hi, I'm Scarlet Rose Westfield. You must be Mike Aviara."

Mike looks at the young girl before him. He gives her a big grin. "Yes, I'm Mike. Good to meet you, Scarlet Rose." He reaches to grab hold of her steady hand. He holds her grip longer than normal.

"You must be Mike." Charles walks towards the front door. "I see you've already met our daughter, Scarlet Rose. I'm Charles. I can't thank you enough for your help. Come on in." Charles reaches to offer a handshake.

"Yes, I do what I can do to help out. I've brought something." He brings his hand forward that up to this point had been held behind him.

"They're beautiful! Scarlet Rose exclaims, "I'll take them." She grabs the red roses from Mike's grasp and hurries away. "Mom, he brought flowers."

"Quite a young lady you've got there," Mike says.

"Yes. She's a good kid. Takes after Cass. I love them both. But, hey, come on in." Charles steps aside to let Mike step forward.

"Nice place," Mike says as he slowly looks around. "Been here a while?"

"Yeah, we bought just at the right time. I wish we could say it was all well planned out, but to be honest, it was purely luck." Charles gives Mike a quick look over and then smiles.

"Where's Cass?"

"She's in the kitchen putting some final touches on dinner. Can I get you a drink?"

Before Mike can answer, he looks up to see Cass slowly walk his way. There is passion in his eyes as he feels the heat from his body rise. His arms move forward ever so slightly to grab hold of her, but he harnesses them in the nick of time. He stays motionless and then a big smile quickly covers his olive complexion face.

"Hello Mike, so glad to see you again." Cass' voice is warm but distant sounding. She extends a hand well before she is close to him to avoid an embrace. "I see you've met Charles and Scarlet Rose."

Mike picks up on the subtleness of her actions and decides to go along for a short time. "Yes, you've got a wonderful family." Then he extends his hand to take hold of hers. He squeezes her hand with sufficient force to keep her locked in his grasp, yet he feels her try to tug away. Satisfied he's made it clear of his attraction to her he lets his hand relax.

She pulls her hand away. Her face flashes annoyance.

Mike easily notices her displeasure but keeps a full smile.

In a passive voice, Cass says, "Charles told me about introducing him to Bent and Brooks. That's very kind of you."

Charles jumps in. "And the interviews today with them and First Floor Solar went very well. They said they would call me later on this week. I feel real confident about the prospects."

Mike says, "I'm sure everything will work out fine."

"How about that drink?" Charles asks.

Ω Ω Ω Ω Ω

To everyone's satisfaction, dinner talk goes smoothly.

"That was terrific. It's been quite a while since I've had homemade food." Mike takes another sip of water.

Scarlet Rose asks, "Where do you eat?"

"Mostly at restaurants, I travel quite a bit. After a while the food at all the restaurants tastes the same."

Scarlet Rose moves onto another basic question, "Do you have a family?"

Before Cass can interrupt, Mike answers. "Not like what you have."

"What does that mean ... I don't understand?"

Cass butts in, "Honey, I think that might be too personal."

Scarlet Rose frowns.

Mike picks up on the situation. "No, that's OK Cass." He turns to Scarlet Rose. "It's just that I travel so much I've never had time to get married and raise a family."

Cass is about to say something but stops short. She remembers Mike saying to her during the reunion that his wife died a while back. Why would he change his story? She keeps that thought private as she fiddles with food on her plate.

"Oh." Scarlet Rose hesitates and then asks another question. "Were you and my mother boyfriend and girlfriend in college?"

Cass feels her face flush. She is not able get out a word.

Charles remains quiet, stunned as well from the question.

Mike saves the day. "Not really boyfriend and girlfriend, just good friends. That's all."

"Oh, I see." Scarlet Rose shrugs her shoulders.

Ω Ω Ω Ω Ω

Later the same night, Cass and Charles lie awake in bed. Neither one can fall asleep.

Charles asks, "What's the matter?"

"Oh, nothing."

"I'm sorry, I should be able to get it up."

"It's not that, so don't worry."

"I should be able to get it up. I feel recharged about the job prospect."

"Don't worry." She turns to face him. "I'll always love you."

"But earlier today I was a different man."

"It happens."

"So there's nothing bothering you?"

Cass hesitates, unsure if she should tell him exactly what is wrong. She tells a partial truth. "I don't know, but I feel something wasn't just right at dinner."

He knows his wife well enough not to get in her face, so he takes it slowly. "I thought everything went smoothly. The food was terrific, as usual, and the conversations went well. Maybe Scarlet Rose got a little too personal with Mike."

She thinks twice before going on, but then gives in. "Maybe it had to do with Scarlet Rose. Maybe that's what's bothering me. I don't know. Am I getting jealous or overprotective of my daughter?"

"She is becoming a young woman, and this is the time when her thoughts run wild. Just like for boys turning into young men."

"So, you don't think there is anything to worry about?"

"If you're thinking about sexual fantasies, there isn't much we can do about that. We can only protect, or try to protect, her from nasty people. But in the end, there's just so much we can do." He pauses, thinking Cass will say something. When she remains quiet, he continues. "Do you want me to say something to Mike?"

Cass' eyes open wide, in a fearful looking way. "No, don't talk with him. I'll speak with Scarlet Rose, girl to girl, about those things. I think that's the best way to handle it."

"If that will ease your mind, then OK."

"You want to try it one more time?" Cass asks.

Charles smiles.

Ω Ω Ω Ω Ω

The next day Charles receives an important phone call.

"Mr. Westfield, this is Denise Cameon from First Floor Solar. How are you today?"

He takes in a deep breath. For the moment he is not sure exactly where he is, an odd sensation temporarily takes over. Quickly he recovers, "Yes, Ms. Cameon, I'm fine."

"That's good to hear. Well, your references checked out wonderfully. Are you still interested in the position?"

Charles' eyes brighten. "Yes, of course."

"That's great. I'm offering you the position as we've previously discussed. Do you accept?"

"Yes, I accept."

"Wonderful. We need to finalize the terms and conditions. Can you come down to my office today or tomorrow to confirm everything?"

"Tha-that's wonderful to hear. Yes, I can be there this afternoon, say at three?"

"That won't work. I've got too many things to finish

before the day is over. How about after hours, say at 5:30?"

"Yes, 5:30 is fine."

"Bring your passport and driver's license with you. There's paperwork to complete. Figure about an hour. I can't imagine it taking longer than that."

"No problem."

"Congratulations, and welcome to First Floor Solar!"

"Yes, I'm very happy to be part of First Floor Solar." He hears the phones disconnect. For a moment he remains still, and then he makes a call to Cass.

The phone rings three times before he hears her outgoing message, so he waits for it to end before he leaves a message of his own. "Cass, I'm going to First Floor Solar late this afternoon at 5:30 to accept a job offer! This is wonderful, and I'm unbelievably happy! We owe much thanks to Mike. I'll talk to you later. I'll be late for dinner but don't hold up on my account. You and Scarlet Rose eat alone. Just warm up whatever you two have when I come home. Love you."

Ω Ω Ω Ω Ω

Charles arrives a little ahead of time at First Floor Solar. He takes a seat in the company's lobby after announcing himself to the receptionist, Jennie. It is 5:20 pm. The office seems empty.

Jennie says, "Hi Mr. Westfield. Denise will be with you shortly. I'll be going home, and there won't be anyone else around after I leave, just you and Denise."

"Thanks." Charles feels all charged up.

After Jennie make the necessary adjustments on the company's phone's lines for the evening, she steps around her reception desk to leave. "Good night Mr. Westfield."

"Have a good evening, Jennie."

A few minutes later Charles sees Denise Cameon, Human Resources Director, slowly walk his way. Her appearance seems different than when he interviewed with her and other staff members. He notices the curves of her body, bouncy breasts, and succulent looking lips. He notices her hips slightly sway from side to side with each step. He wonders if she had worn a skirt just above the knees when they first met, like the one she has on now. She looks attractive to him. He tries to put those thoughts out of his mind, but the closer she gets the more intent his stare.

"Good to see you again, Charles. We are very happy you will be joining the First Floor Solar family." She smiles brightly and extends her hand for a shake.

Charles notices a small but noticeable gap between her two front teeth. He wonders why he had not noticed it before. He says, "Yes, I'm very happy to join First Floor Solar."

"Follow me. You have a few forms to complete, nothing unusual. You understand." She turns with Charles close behind.

Moments later she says to Charles, "Take that seat." She points to one of two empty chairs around a circular table in her office. "I'll walk you through the forms you have to complete." She closes the door.

Charles notices papers on top of the table, and an opened laptop computer. He does not give much importance to a green light at the top-center of the laptop.

"There's paperwork to complete, nothing unusual. Did you bring your passport and driver's license?"

"Yes, I have it right here." Charles dips his hand into a dark chocolate colored briefcase to pull out the two documents."

"That's a Longchamp, isn't it?" She reaches to touch the briefcase. "I just love the touch of soft leather. I guess I'm just the feeling type, you know, best suited for a Human Resources career." She glances away from the briefcase to make eye contact with Charles.

"Yeah, I guess so. My wife's a Human Resources Director."

"Isn't that interesting? Maybe I've met her at one of our Society meetings?"

"Could be, her name is Cass, formally Cassandra."

"Umm, that doesn't ring a bell. There are so many members."

Charles isn't sure if it is his turn to so say something, so he decides to forge ahead. "Here are the two documents, passport and driver's license." He places them on the top of the small table.

"Of course, we should get started on the paperwork or we'll be here all night. And you don't want to be late for dinner with your family." She takes the two documents, looks them over, and transfers information onto a few forms as Charles watches. "That should do it." She looks at the photos inside the two documents, and then looks directly at Charles. "These photos don't do you justice. You're much handsomer in person." She glances one more time at the photos and then hands them back to Charles.

He begins to feel a little uncomfortable. He twists his body in the chair, grabs the two documents, and puts them back into his briefcase.

"Now it's your turn." She moves her chair closer to him, almost rubbing her arm with his. She slides one document his way and points a finger at the form. "This is the application form. Just follow the directions to complete it fully. No empty spaces." She glances up with another bright smile.

Charles feels the urge to move away but resists. The lilac smell of her perfume keeps him in place. He takes another deep swallow.

Denise continues. "This is your health care form. Complete it fully as well." She slides the form close to him.

Charles notices her long fingernails, brushed to a high gloss.

"Just two more forms to go." Denise breathes out sufficiently loud and long for Charles to hear what he thinks is a groan. "Then there is the secrecy and confidentiality form, and finally the EEOC form. They're all self explanatory so I think you won't have any difficulty. I'll leave you alone to complete them but I'll only be a shout away. I'll check back with you in twenty minutes. OK?" She covers his hand with her hand.

Charles feels his body stiffen. "Yes, that's fine. Twenty minutes should do it."

As Denise stands, her leg brushes against Charles' leg. She remains motionless for a few seconds and then leaves her office.

Now alone, Charles shakes his head, confused with her behavior. "Was she coming on to me?" He thinks for a few seconds. "Or am I just overly sensitive right now?" He shoves the chair previously used by Denise away from him and decides to forget the idea. Then he starts on finishing the forms.

Elsewhere, Denise makes her way to the ladies restroom. She pulls out her cell phone to make a call. "This is me." She listens for a few seconds. "Everything is going fine. I'll send it to you once I'm done." She listens again. "Of course he's nervous. Wouldn't you be if you were in his shoes?" She laughs. "OK, maybe not you specifically, but you know what I mean." There is another laugh. "Just make sure you deposit the money as agreed." Her face turns somber. "No, I wasn't implying anything, just reminding you of our deal. That's all." She grins. "Ciao baby." Once the phone disconnects, she looks at herself in the mirror. Denise ruffles her hair just a wee-bit, unfastens two buttons on her red blouse, and removes her panties. She puckers her lips and says, "The last dance." She wiggles her hips and returns to her office to check up on Charles.

As she walks into the office, Charles says, "That wasn't so bad." Charles feels invigorated and self-confident all over again.

Denise says, "Great, let me just review them to make sure you haven't missed anything." She notices her chair has been returned to its original location. She smiles to herself and takes a seat. Denise takes a few minutes to scan the documents. "Yes, everything is completed." She turns to face Charles, "Your start date is next Monday.

Congratulations." She extends her hand to shake as she smiles his way.

Charles automatically reciprocates the move. He feels her firm grasp that lasts a little longer than expected, and then she loosens her hold. He is the first to pull away. "Thank you very much."

"I'm sure you're going to enjoy it here."

As he looks at Denise, he notices something out of place but can't put his finger on it. He shrugs off the thought. "Yes, I think so as well."

"Are there any questions you'd like to ask me?"

Charles watches Denise slowly cross her long slender legs. He tries to glance away but his eyes stay focused on her legs. Then he notices the unfastened two buttons. He feels his body heat up. Finally he looks up at her face. He clears his throat and says, "No, I think you've covered everything. Is there something I should have asked?"

She flutters her eyes and then replies, "I don't know, is there?" She smiles, waits for a response.

Charles is clueless and motionless.

She continues. "Can I do anything for you?" She leans forward, touches his knee with her hand, and squeezes it slightly. She keeps eye contact all the while.

He looks at her hand on his knee. He wants to pull away, to tell her she is out of line, but he does not at first. He feels himself get worked-up. He tries to look at her face, but his eyes stop to get a good look at her cleavage. Finally he manages to ask, "What are you doing?"

"What do you think?"

"You're flirting with me. Is this part of the orientation?"

"It's OK. There is nothing to worry about. We're alone, just you and me." Her hand stays on his knee.

Charles is tongue-tied for the moment. Words stay hidden from his consciousness. He cannot move his body to break away. Even if he could get away, he wonders if he would want to. Then he manages to find words. "You are flirting with me and this isn't right." He moves his knee out of reach of her hand. "Don't do that again."

She wiggles her eyebrows and puckers her juicy looking lips. "Oh Charles, we're both adults." She stands, spreads her legs slightly, and puts her hands on her hips.

"No, I mean it."

"Don't you find me attractive?"

He looks over her body and then forces himself to glance away. "That has nothing to do with it. It's not right."

She is persistent. "It has everything to do with it. I have an idea that I think you'll like." She steps closer to Charles as he remains motionless.

Ten minutes later Denise says, "Well, that was some ride." She stays on top of him and wiggles a little.

Charles is not sure where he is or what just happened. It all seems fuzzy and surreal. Then he extends his arms towards her shoulders. "Get off!"

"Whatever." She moves away from him.

Charles zips up his pants and clumsily leaves Denise's office. He walks in a robotic-like manner, numb of feelings, and void of clear thoughts.

He manages to find his way to the outside where the fresh air starts to ignite human-like emotions. While he is confused about what just happened, he also feels shame and regret. He does not know what to do or whom to turn to. Definitely he is not about to tell Cass what just happened. The whole incident is unbelievable to him and came totally out of the blue.

Once Denise is alone, she closes the door and puts on her clothes. She reaches for her cell phone to call the same private number, and then says, "It's done."

Ω Ω Ω Ω Ω

The drive home is painful as Charles thinks about what has just happened. No matter how he dissects what has occurred, he comes back to the same conclusion … stupidity. Never-the-less he tries to analyze it one more time.

He says to himself that infidelity is done by the other guy who does not love his wife, not by someone like him who could not live without his wife. He knows a few couples who have gone through tough times that stretched the faithfulness of their marriage, but as far as he knows, betrayal was not part of it. It would be different if his wife did it first, and he was trying to even the score. But it is nothing like that, or even close to it. He believes Cass would never violate their bond, not for an instant.

Granted Denise is one hell of a good looking woman, very sensuous, but he has known many others just like her. Yet, in the end, nothing happened, just a few idle thoughts here and there. In fact, he has no desire to be alone with Denise ever again. As far as he is concerned she is out of his mind.

However avoiding seeing and talking with the company's Human Resources Director will be impossible. There will be times when he will have to discuss employee relations issues, and even matters pertaining to him. No, he has to be careful around her. There is too much at risk.

Then something pops into his head. He could resign right now even before starting the first day of work. That would solve it all. He gives that some thought, but decides it to be foolish. No, he will go to work on Monday, but he will be very careful, prudent, and sensible. Hell, he needs the job.

He considers if he should tell Cass about the whole thing, to bring it out in the open. There are advantages to get rid of the secret from the woman he so desperately loves. The biggest benefit is trust. Get it out in the open, apologize, and promise never to do it again.

There are several disadvantages. The main ones are contempt and censure. Even if Cass doesn't leave him, she would continually pass judgment on him. He would constantly feel it 24-7. That is something he is not sure he would be able to live with.

And, of course, there is his daughter. Scarlet Rose would never forgive him … never in a million years … that he cheated on her mother.

He wonders what other guys would do if they were in his shoes. He suspects most men probably think it is only human nature for married men to be pleased to discover that an attractive woman has sexual desires for them. Sex can get boring with the same partner, and even get extinct. He admits it temporarily happened to him and Cass just a while back. But the real question he asks himself is would most men go through with it or simple enjoy the thought of hooking up with an eye-catching woman. And how many men, if they did it once, would continue doing it again? He has no real answer, and for that matter, it does not matter what other men would or would not do. He did it once and now he has to figure out what to do next.

He stops for a red light to give more time to think about the situation. He looks to his right where he sees an elderly man sitting behind the wheel of a late model car. In the passenger's seat next to him is a woman who appears to be of similar age. Charles assumes they have been married for quite a while. He wonders if either one of them has cheated on the other. Charles then turns to face forward.

He wonders what it was about him that caused Denise to come on to him the way she did. Did he send her a message of some sort that said, come hither, or was it something else? Since he has never had this happen to him before, he questions that he is the cause. He figures it certainly wasn't his celebrity status! He laughs a little, more of nervous reaction than anything else. That brings him to another round of questions.

If it wasn't him, then who or what could it be? He frowns, and then continues wondering. Is Denise so consumed by sex that any new man who enters her life is fair game?

He pauses and then lets out another nervous grunt. Preposterous or maybe not. He has heard of men and women who can't get enough sex that they prey on anyone who is available. They even risk their jobs and other relationships. He wonders if that is the answer. Lucky me. He snickers. But she is as beautiful as she is evil, and God, is she ever beautiful.

A blaring car horn takes him out of his thought

process. He checks the signal light. It is now green, so he moves forward.

He continues to wonder how something like this could happen to him. He is not a man's-man, just a person, and an ordinary person at that. No fame, no glory, and no hangers-on who covet his attention. Is there something he doesn't know but should know? Does someone else know something that they are not telling him?

Oh, hell, he screwed up. That's all there is to it. But he has to tell Cass all about it. She'll forgive him, he just knows it.

Up ahead is another signal light. The light is red so he stops. This time he looks to his left where he sees a young couple stroll hand-and-hand on the sidewalk. They stop for a second to kiss. Charles wonders how long their relationship will last before one of them deceives the other.

Ω Ω Ω Ω

During dinner on the same day, Cass appears more upbeat than Charles. "We had to wait for you to come home. We couldn't have dinner by ourselves and not celebrate with you. You should be very pleased with yourself. I'm so proud of you." She raises a glass of water to celebrate."

"Yeah dad, hip-hip-hurrah." Scarlet Rose joins in the celebration.

Charles forces a smile, nods a few times as acknowledgment. He remains quiet.

"What's troubling you? You should be jubilant," Cass asks.

He clears his throat. "I guess it hasn't hit me yet. Let's face it, it happened so unexpectedly."

"Sure, but that's no reason to ignore the outcome."

Scarlet Rose silently listens as she takes another bite of broccoli.

Charles feels his throat constrict, so he reaches to take a sip of water. A few drops cling to his chin.

Cass leans forward to wipe off the loose water beads. "Is there a lot of travel that will take you away from us for long periods of time? Do we have to relocate? What is it?"

"I love steamed broccoli," Scarlet Rose says. She takes another bite of food. "I could eat an entire meal of broccoli." Her smile is genuine as she looks at the plate of food in front of her.

Charles and Cass glance at their daughter. Proud smiles cover their faces.

Charles then looks at Cass. "I think it just happened so quickly. I'm alright and nothing will change with our family." Then Charles half-heartedly says, "I guess we've got to thank Mike for the job."

Cass turns to look at Charles. "But you don't seem all that enthused."

Charles puckers his lips to keep silent.

Scarlet Rose says, "I think Mike is a good friend."

Charles looks at her but keeps quiet.

Cass frowns, and stares at her daughter. "Really?"

"Yeah." Scarlet Rose looks up at her parents, surprised to see mild shock on their faces. "What's wrong?"

"Why did you say that?" Cass asks.

"I just think he's a good friend," Scarlet Rose naively answers.

"Is it because he helped your dad find a job, is that why you think he's a good friend?"

Scarlet Rose answers, "Yeah, that's part of it."

Cass asks, "So, there's more to it."

"Sure."

Cass takes in a deep breath. She feels her stomach tighten. "Please tell us."

She looks directly at her mother. "He's met me after school and we've talked."

"What!" Cass' eyes widen with panic. She glances at Charles to see his worried expression.

Calmly Scarlet Rose says, "Yeah, we've talked about stuff."

Cass asks, "What stuff?"

Scarlet Rose says, "He wanted to know what subjects I enjoy in school, what my extracurricular activities are. You know, those sorts of things. He's been interested in what I want to do in my life, you know, whether I want to go to college or whatever."

Charles jumps into the conversation. "When did this start?"

Their daughter looks to the ceiling for a split second and then faces her father, "The day after he was here for dinner."

"Why didn't you tell us about this?"

She shrugs her shoulders, "Because there's nothing to tell." Scarlet frowns, troubled by her parents' reaction, "I don't get it. We just talked about stuff."

Charles adds, "Mike is a nice man. We all know that. But, when a grown man meets with a young girl without telling her parents or even asking for permission, then you can imagine how surprised we are. Don't you agree?"

"Hmm, I guess so. I never thought about it that way." She gets back to eating the remaining broccoli on her plate.

"Honey, your dad and I have had numerous talks about meeting alone with strangers. There are some very bad people out there who could harm you. You do remember, don't you?"

"Yes." Scarlet Rose looks up. "You've told me to walk away, to say no, and to tell another adult about it. Yes, I remember."

"Then, sweetie, why didn't you tell your father or me about meeting with Mike?"

"He's not a stranger." Scarlet Rose frowns.

Cass and Charles look at each other. They see worry in each other's eyes.

"I think I'll give him a call to find out what's going on," Charles says.

"Yes, please do." Cass then turns towards her daughter. "There's nothing to worry about. Your father and I are just surprised that he would meet with you and not tell us about it. It's all very unusual."

Scarlet Rose asks, "Am I in trouble?"

Cass answers, "No you're not."

Scarlet Rose wonders, "So, can I still see Mike?"

Cass asks, "When is the next time?"

Their daughter says, "He said he'd be traveling and not for another week or so."

Cass takes in a deep breath of relief and now seems a bit more settled. "We'll have it all sorted out by then. But do your father and me a favor. Tell us when he contacts you again, and don't see him until we are made aware. Will you do that for us?"

Scarlet Rose shrugs her shoulders, "Sure, no problem."

Charles adds, "Even if he says he's already informed us, you should tell us just the same."

"Got it." Scarlet Rose nods her head and smiles. "Pass the broccoli, please."

Ω Ω Ω Ω Ω

Later the same night, Cass and Charles lay close together, wide awake, in bed. Both of them stare at the white ceiling.

"You want to try it again?"

She continues to gaze upward. "I'm sorry, but I'm not in the mood."

"What are you thinking about?" he asks her.

"I can't believe Mike would do this without telling us first." She wonders if he is feeling the same way, so she asks. "What do you think?"

"Same with me. I know he was instrumental in getting me the job, but, being alone with our daughter without giving us a heads up is beyond my comprehension. It's creepy."

"It's not as if he is her uncle, cousin, or close friend. I'd have an easier time understanding that, but, no, not this way."

"Well, I'll call him in the morning. I'm sure there is a good explanation."

Cass asks, "Is there anything else bothering you?"

"No, why do you ask?"

Cass turns to face Charles, "Let's try it one more time."

Ω Ω Ω Ω Ω

The next morning Charles calls Mike. The phone rings a few times before he hears an outgoing phone message. "This is Mike Aviara. I'm traveling and not able to take your call. Please leave a voice message and I'll return the call as soon as possible. Have a great day."

Beep.

"Hey, Mike. This is Charles Westfield. I just want to thank you again for helping me get the job at First Floor Solar. I start Monday. You've been a great help. When you get a chance, I'd like to talk with you about something, specifically, about you and Scarlet Rose. She's told us about your meetings, and well, to be honest, Cass and I are a little concerned. I'm sure you can clarify it all. So, give me a call as soon as you can. And, again, thanks for your help."

Mike listens in, grins, and figures he will call back when he is in the mood, whenever that might be. No need to clarify anything to anyone until he is ready. And he is not ready to tell anyone about his plans at the moment.

Ω Ω Ω Ω Ω

The State Street Restaurant is an off-the-beaten path luncheon spot that was popular at one time but less so today. Cass and Iris sit across from each other.

Cass says, "Thanks for joining me for lunch."

Iris looks around the place. "I haven't been here in quite a while. Did we miss the luncheon crowd?"

"No. Too many newer places have opened up recently. Anyway I don't want to be rushed."

"Sure, what's up? You look frazzled."

"We're the best of friends. This has to be between the two of us. OK?"

"You've got my word on it."

Cass says, "This is the first time I've had the nerve to talk to you, or anyone for that matter, about the reunion."

"To be honest, I've been dying to ask you about it, but, well, I figured you'd tell me when you were ready. What happened?"

Cass takes in a deep breath of air, swallows, and takes a sip of water. "I feel as if my life is unraveling. I don't know what to do?"

Iris' eyes widen with alarm. "You can tell me anything. Just take your time." She pats Cass' hand for encouragement.

"Do you remember when I told you about Mike Aviara, the guy who sent me such a persuasive e-mail about the class reunion?"

Iris nods without saying a word.

"Well, I had dinner with him."

"That's innocent enough." Iris looks at Cass' troubled face. "Oh, there's more. Go on."

"He's back in my life and I'm terrified."

"I'm listening."

Cass finds the strength to take in another needed breath of air and slowly let it float away. "I had an affair with him during the reunion. I tried to control myself, but I couldn't. It actually happened twice. I can't believe how easy it was to get back in the frame of mind of being with him in college." She stares at Iris, looking for comfort.

Iris silently stares at Cass, disappointment and shock cover her face.

"Don't say that you told me so. Please, don't say it."

"What do you want me to say, that it's OK to sleep with someone who's not your husband?"

"No I don't, but it did happen! I'm trying to forget about him and move on but there are some complications."

Iris takes in a deep breath and continues to look at Cass without blinking.

"He won't go away in spite of me telling him to get out of my life. He's obsessed with me." Cass takes a sip of water. "Don't be quiet, say something!"

"I'm not sure I know what to say. Is there more you want to tell me?"

"Yes, there's more."

"Oh my gosh." Iris puts her hands to her mouth.

"No, I'm not pregnant, if that's what you're thinking."

Iris settles her hands on the table and blows out a sigh of relief. "Well, that's good."

"It's something worse, something that I hoped would never happen, but I'm beginning to realize my worst nightmare. I'm terrified. I don't want to lose my family."

"What possibly could be so bad that you're so afraid of?"

Cass looks away and spots a waiter standing a few feet away.

He nods his head and then he walks towards her.

"Good afternoon ladies. Can I offer you something to drink?"

"Just iced tea," Cass says.

"Same here," adds Iris.

"Perfect. Here are your menus. I'll be right back with your drinks."

Alone again with Iris, Cass continues. "He's getting personally involved in my family."

"What do you mean?"

"He introduced Charles to an executive search firm that eventually led to an interview with a local company that eventually hired him. And now Charles thinks he's a great guy."

"What's the problem with that? I'd think you and Charles would be delighted. I don't get it."

"Then, behind Charles' and my backs he's met with Scarlet Rose after school! He's talked with her about what she wants for a career, how her classes are going, and what her extracurricular activities are! I mean, he's acting as if he is part of the family! I'm freaking out!"

"Oh, that would creep me out."

"Even Scarlet Rose thinks of him as a good friend!"

"Have you told him to back off?"

"I told him after the first and second times we were together that we would not see each other again. Then, Charles left a voice message to ask about his secret meetings with Scarlet Rose, but all he got was Mike's answering service. We haven't been able to settle this."

"That's not good. Is there anything else?"

"Yes."

Before either Cass or Iris is able to continue, the waiter returns. "Here are your iced teas. Have you decided what you'll have for lunch?" He takes out a hand-held device to electronically order their luncheon requests.

Iris looks at Cass who shrugs her shoulders. Then she says, "Do you have spinach salads?"

"Yes, of course. Is that what you'd like?"

"Yes, but without croutons. And put the dressing on the side."

"OK." He presses a few buttons on the hand-held device. Then he turns to Cass, "What will you have?"

"The same."

"Fine, that makes it easy." He finishes off ordering the food and steps away.

Iris returns to their earlier conversation. "You said there was more to tell me."

"He's become very possessive. It's as if he wants to own me. I'm scared what he could do."

"You've got to be clearer."

"I think he's obsessed with me."

"Could it be mutual?"

"That's ridiculous! I'm not fixated on him!"

"OK, still I think that's something you have to come to grips with. But, go on."

"You're wrong." Cass pauses and then continues. "When we were first together at the reunion I interpreted his attention as flattering."

"Of course, why wouldn't you?"

"Yes, I agree, it was a great feeling to know that someone other than my husband desired me. In some way I didn't want to lose that feeling. But I now realize that was a big mistake."

"Oh."

"He seems more determined to keep it going on indefinitely. I feel shameful and guilty as it is, but if he gets what he wants, he'll ruin my marriage. I can't let that happen! I'd do anything to shield this from Charles and Scarlet Rose, anything!"

"If he's stalking you, call the cops."

"I don't think that's a good idea. I'd have to explain more than I'm willing to. Charles would find out and matters would be worse."

"If you believe Charles would stand by you knowing the truth, then tell him everything."

The waiter appears. "Here are your salads. Is there something else I can do?"

Cass looks at the plate of food in front of her.

Iris says, "That should be all. Thank you."

"Yes, I'll come back in a while to check up. Enjoy." The waiter leaves.

Cass says, "I don't have the nerve to tell Charles. Even if he said he forgave me I'd still feel condemned. I know our relationship would change for the worse."

"And how do you think it will turn out if you don't tell him?"

"I'm beginning to believe that sometimes secrets are left unsaid." Cass pauses. "And there's Scarlet Rose? She'd never forgive me as her mother for sleeping around."

"There's a price to pay for keeping secrets."

"I know."

"It's too bad he won't go away forever."

"Yeah, that would be ideal, gone, once and for all."

Ω Ω Ω Ω Ω

It is Saturday morning. The sky is clear of clouds and the air smells fresh.

However, Charles is down in the dumps. He feels defeated, unable to stop thinking of the recent indiscretion with Denise. He does not know how to escape the emotion. He is troubled and needs to talk with someone in confidence. He spots Joe clipping a branch from a tree in his front yard. He walks towards his neighbor. "Got a minute?"

Joe looks up. "Sure, what's up?" He lowers the clipper.

"I need to talk with you about something. It's important."

Joe looks at his neighbor's worried eyes and realizes something real bad is troubling his friend. "By all means." He places the clipper on the ground. "Here or some other place?"

Charles swallows deeply, about to take back the request. "If it's not a good time, maybe later."

"No, no. Now is good. Let's take a walk down the street." Joe puts his hand on his friend's shoulder. "Come on, what's on your mind?"

Charles starts out. "This has never happened to me before, ever before, as God is my judge." His head tilts toward the sidewalk, purposely ignoring looking squarely at Joe.

"There's always a first time for everything." Joe tries to lighten the conversation, but when he sees fright in the face of Charles he immediately realizes the approach is in poor taste. "What I mean is we all do something for the first time." When he sees Charles' face remain frightened he realizes he is making matters worse, so he decides to let Charles talk. He turns his head away from Charles.

"Have you ever done something you knew was wrong but did it anyway, or maybe just couldn't stop yourself?"

"Are you talking about legally wrong? Remember I'm an attorney."

"No, not legally wrong."

Joe smiles a little thinking back a few times where he messed up. "Of course, I can't imagine anyone not getting in a jam one time or another. It happens to all of us."

"I've been quite conservative most of my life. I've played by the rules, even being honest with my income taxes. No fudging. I wish I could say it was the way I was brought up, but my father wasn't exactly a role model." Charles looks at Joe. "It always hasn't led to the optimal results, but at least I've been able to live with myself. Know what I mean?"

Joe thinks he knows where the conversation is headed, but keeps the suspicion to himself. "Yeah, I know what you mean."

"I remember a time in high school. I was playing varsity basketball. It was against our main rival. The score was even and time was running out. The ball came to me for the final shot. I stepped back a little to give myself room for a three-pointer when I noticed my foot was on the out-of-bounds line. Nobody noticed I was out-of-bounds, only me. I could have taken the shot anyway, but I tossed the ball to the ref saying I was out-of-bounds. My coach and teammates were angry with me. The fans booed me. But I thought I was just doing the right thing by following the rules."

Joe's eyes widen, astonished to hear the story. "No kidding?" It is all he is able to think of saying.

Charles sees a surprised expression from Joe. "I know it doesn't sound true, but it really happened. Honest."

"I believe you, really I do."

"We eventually won the game, but everybody, I mean everybody, kept reminding me of what I did. I guess that should have been a life-lesson event. It's OK to break the rules if you don't get caught."

Joe keeps quiet, but nods his head just the same.

Charles continues. "I broke another rule recently, and I'm still struggling with how to handle it. That's why I need your help."

"As I said, my expertise is the legal side but I'm here to listen and maybe have an idea or two."

"This has to be kept quiet. You've got to promise me regardless of what happens. Will you promise me?"

Joe nods his head, yes. "Absolutely, you've got my word on it."

"I got a job offer and I start work this Monday."

"That's terrific! Congratulations." Joe is enthusiastic, but wonders what the dilemma his neighbor is facing.

"Well, I'm not so sure it's all that great. When I explain, you'll get the picture."

"I'm listening. Go on."

Charles clears his throat. "Cass' college friend, a guy she went to school with, gave me the lead. She and Mike Aviara, that's his name, evidently talked during her reunion. She must have mentioned to him that I was looking for work. And then clear out of the blue, he called me to set up a job interview with an executive search firm who passed me onto a local company, First Floor Solar. Cass and I were quite surprised that this guy, who Cass hasn't seen or heard from since graduation, did this for me. I mean … how many times do people go out of their way to help out another person? Huh?" He pauses.

Joe is not sure he is expected to respond, so he keeps quiet.

Charles continues. "Anyway, the job interviews went

so well that they offered me a job. I accepted it." He clears his throat and his voice quivers. "Then this was when my troubles began." He feels himself get emotionally worked up so he pauses to calm down.

Joe hears Charles' voice tremble so he says, "It's OK, take your time."

"I had to schedule a time to meet their HR Director to fill out the new hire paperwork. I had met her before during the interview process and everything seemed just fine. But when I met with her, one-on-one to complete the forms, she was very different. I mean … very different."

Joe's interest peaks but he keeps quiet.

"I won't get into the details, but after the paperwork was complete, she came on to me, big time. I was shocked and I resisted a little at first, not but entirely. I don't know if I could have refused to give in to her sexual advances even if I wanted to. The bottom line is I didn't. I stepped out-of-bounds and I haven't told anyone about it, except now you. I took the shot and it went into the basket. No one knows, not even Cass."

Joe waits for a question, but when Charles remains silent, Joe says, "So you had sex with her."

"Yes."

"Well, what do you want to do now?"

"That's it, I don't know."

"Do you want to continue having an affair with her?"

"God, no! I love Cass!"

Joe says, "Then it's quite simple."

"What's that?"

Joe looks directly at Charles. "Keep it quiet. Don't

tell anyone, I mean no one. This stays between us, just you and me."

"I don't know if I can do that."

"Can or want?"

"Huh?"

"You can do anything you want to do. As I see it you've got two choices. One is you tell Cass, and the other is you don't. It's quite simple. Don't make this more complex than it really is."

"What if Cass finds out? What then, what would I do if she finds out and confronts me?"

"You deny it. Sometimes secrets are best kept from those you love."

"What is she finds out but doesn't say anything?"

"The same, don't say anything. Total truth is not all it's cracked up to be. Take my word on it."

"I've got to be honest with you. I can't help thinking about the HR Director and me getting it on in her office."

"Why?"

"It was one of the most exhilarating and frightening things I've ever done. Maybe it was the single most."

"It sounds as if you'd like to experience it again."

"Don't be foolish. I'd never do it again with her."

"Then keep it locked up in a very secure place where no one has access."

"Hmm."

"What about her? Do you think she wants more of you?"

"I can't imagine. She's very good looking and I bet she could be with any man she wants. I'm an ordinary guy. There's nothing special about me."

"Come on Charles, there had to be something special about getting it on with you."

"No way, I don't believe that for one second."

"I wouldn't conclude that so fast. Just follow my thinking for a minute. If there's nothing special about you or if you're not suspicious about her intentions, then you've got to ask, why you? Why did she chose you?"

Charles answers, "Great question. Maybe she's the type of person who's obsessed with having sex, and I was available."

"How sure are you?"

Charles pauses before he answers. "To be honest, I really don't know. What I'm really concerned about is that I might have additional problems with her."

Joe frowns, "And what's that?"

"We'll be working for the same company, and our offices will be in the same general area. I'll probably see her almost every day, but definitely when there are employee concerns, in addition to my own. I'm going to have to talk with her on personnel matters. There is no way to get around it." Charles feels his body tighten.

"I see what you mean."

Charles elaborates. "I even thought of quitting before I start on Monday, but threw that idea out of the window. I need to get back to work, and I'd have to explain it to Cass."

"Hmm, it sounds as if you've already solved the problem."

Charles frowns without a comment.

"You are not prepared to tell Cass."

"What a mess I've put myself in."

"It's only a mess if you think of it that way. You can only do what you are prepared to do."

"So you don't think I should tell Cass about it?"

"That's my advice, but it's up to you."

"I know that, but what would you do?"

"Me? I'd lock it up in a safe so secure that no one could get into it, even me, even if I changed my mind. That's what I would do."

"I'm not sure I can do that?"

"Like I said, it's up to you, but you've only got two choices."

CHAPTER 4

"Mr. Aviara, I finished the job." Lou D'Amico sets aside the cigar on the edge of a wooden table. He puts on reading glasses to make sure he is accurate. His boss is adamant about getting things right the first time. There are no second chances and his boss has a history of losing his temper when things do not go his way. "How far back do you wanna know?"

"From the beginning, I want to know everything about her."

"Here goes." Lou clears his throat. "She's a descendant of the Iroquois nation who lived in Canada and New York. There were at least five tribes who lived there, the Mohawk, Oneida, Onondaga, Cayuga, and Seneca. She's Mohawk. They had an interestin' approach to war. They took prisoners and either adopted them into their tribe or else sacrificed them." He lets out a chuckle.

Mike brusquely interrupts. "Move it along, I want to know about her."

"OK, understood." Lou reorders the papers in front of him. "The family's original name of several generations ago was changed from somethin' I can't pronounce to a name that translates to somethin' like Handsome, and then the next generation changed it to Hopeland, and then another change was to Ponytail. Two more changes happened, one to Decanter, and then to Horizon until she married Charles Westfield, her current husband. Her parents were somethin' else. Do you wanna know?"

"Oh, hell, sure, but make it short Lou."

Lou takes a puff from the cigar and lets the smoke out slowly. While still holding the cigar in his hand, he continues. "Jonathan Decanter married Eva Lynn Rye. Jonathan and Eva Lynn were married for seven years. Durin' that time they had Cassandra, officially Cassandra Lilia Decanter. A few years later, when Cassandra Lilia was about four years old, Jonathan filed for divorce. Evidently, Eva Lynn liked to play the field with younger men and she got caught. She was also into drugs and crap. When they divorced, Jonathan got full custody of Cassandra Lilia but Eva Lynn was not happy one bit. OK so far?"

"Yeah, yeah, move it along."

"OK." Lou takes another puff from the cigar and then goes on. "Her father was a church minister. He wanted Cassandra Lilia to have a good mother, so he remarried. This time he married a woman about ten years younger than him, Mary Ann Anderson. It seems like the women in his life all had middle names. I think that's funny." He pauses to hear from Mike.

"I don't give a fuck what you think is funny. Anyway most people have middle names."

"Yes Mr. Aviara." Lou swallows deeply, and then continues. "One night while Jonathan and Mary Ann slept in one room, and Cassandra Lilia in another room, somebody put a slug into his head. His wife claimed she never heard the gun go off and Cassandra Lilia said she thought she saw someone open her bedroom door sometime in the night but wasn't sure. She thought maybe it was just a dream. Anyway, Mary Ann was suspected of killing her husband. She'd receive two hundred thou from a life insurance policy if her husband's death was by natural causes. Another life policy was written on her in case something happened to her. In that case Jonathan would collect. If something happened to both parents at the same time, there was a third policy of the same amount that would go to Cassandra Lilia. Mary Ann never got one penny since her husband was shot point blank while he slept. I guess that doesn't represent a natural death." He thinks it is humorous so he laughs, and then continues. "Cassandra Lilia went to pieces because she and her dad were real close. So far, so good?"

"Yeah yeah, go on."

"OK." Lou takes one more puff from the cigar and as he lets the smoke fill the room he resets it on the corner of the table. "After Jonathan divorced Eva Lynn, she supposedly told her neighbors that she'd get her child back regardless of what it took. When Jonathan was killed, some of the neighbors automatically assumed that Eva Lynn did him in but others thought that Mary Ann put him away. But, there was no evidence to prove anythin', so no one was ever tried for Jonathan's death. But somebody had to do it, know what I mean? Anyway, as far as I know, the case is still open. With her father now dead and the outlook of bein' returned to her mother, who she didn't like one bit, Cassandra Lilia took off. There is no record of Eva Lynn tryin' to find her."

"Are you saying she simply disappeared?"

"Yeah, but only for a short time. This is where the story is a little fuzzy. The next thing I found out was that she was in a Catholic orphanage for a short time, and then later adopted by a family. Their name is Horizon. The Catholic orphanage keeps their records tight, real tight, and I wasn't able to get any more information about what happened durin' that short time. The Horizon family members are all dead. There was just a father and mother. They died in a car accident."

Mike coldly says, "Shit happens."

"Yes Mr. Aviara, it sure does."

"What else is there?"

"As a kid, she was interested in all sorts of sports, you know like soccer and basketball, but she really liked baseball. She didn't wanna play with other girls. Maybe she thought she was better than them. I don't really know. Anyway she changed her appearance just enough and tried out to become part of a boy's baseball team, part of the Little League in the area where she lived. She didn't tell anybody about it. Anyway, she made the team as a starter shortstop. The boy she beat out for the position got real angry about not gettin' the spot so he did some snoopin' on his own. When he found out she was a girl, the kid reported her to the coach that she wasn't a boy but a girl. She finally got booted off the team."

"Lou, what's the point of the story?"

He hesitates. A few beads of perspiration appear on his forehead. "I think it shows how determined she was to get what she wanted."

"Yeah, whatever, go on."

"The rest is simple. She just tried to fit in, you know,

just stay below the radar, to get through each day without much notice."

"Hmm."

"Then she and you met in college, and, well, I don't think I need to get into that."

"Good decision. What happened after college?"

"Well, there's one thing you might be interested in that happened during her senior year in college?"

"What's that?"

"We know that you left college for family matters but finished your degree on-line. But you might not know that Cassandra Lilia was pregnant at the end of her senior year. She graduated and then gave birth to a girl that she named Scarlet Rose. Father is unknown."

Mike quickly interrupts. "I didn't know that. Go on."

"She moved around a little and then she met Charles Westfield."

"Yeah yeah, what else?"

"Cassandra Lilia told Charles that her husband died shortly after Scarlet Rose was born. He accepted that as truth and they married. There doesn't seem to be any problems with their marriage, except for a while when he was unemployed. Things seem to be settled down now since he just took a position with a company titled First Floor Solar. That's about it, Mr. Aviara. Do you have any questions?"

"Not now, maybe later. What's the story with Charles Westfield?"

"Long version or short one?"

"Condense it for now. If I have any questions, I'll ask."

Lou glances at the lit cigar on the corner of the table, and then he grabs it to take a big puff. He holds the smoke inside his lungs for a short time and then lets it slowly escape. He resets the cigar on the corner of the table. He begins the report. "His grandfather was a coalminer in Pennsylvania who died at thirty-seven from a big ... I mean ... really big ... minin' accident that killed him and ten other miners. The company that owned the mine paid off the survivors but continued minin' in the same unsafe conditions. That's how it was done then." He clears his throat and then continues. "His grandmother died a few years later of unknown causes. But before they died they had four children, two boys and two girls. One boy died before he turned one while the other boy lived until he was forty-three. Each of the two girls married at a young age to guys that promised to take them away from the neighborhood to start a new life. The one boy who lived stayed close by his mother, quit high school before he graduated to earn money as a laborer. This kid turned out to become Charles' father, Alfred. After his mother died, Alfred married Eloise and they had Charles and a younger girl. Alfred was not a positive influence on his son."

Mike is quick to ask, "How do you know that?"

"I really don't know for sure, but I found out he was rarely around to see the kid grow up."

Mike disagrees. "That doesn't prove anything! Lots of kids don't have fathers who are a positive influence, but they still grow up to be OK!"

"Yes Mr. Aviara I see what you mean."

In a loud voice Mike orders, "Go on!"

Lou takes in a deep breath, smacks his lips, and continues. "Anyway, he worked and drank a lot. The girl got pregnant at an early age but didn't know the father. She eventually gave her child up for adoption and stayed with her mother until the mother died from alcoholism." He shakes his head and then adds a personal observation. "I guess you can say the odds were against Charles to make his life worthwhile."

"What's your point? The odds are against all of us, you and me included! You've got to take what you want no matter how you do it!" Mike is out of breath. "Go on!"

"Yes Mr. Aviara, I see your point." Lou's eyes widen from the confrontational sound of Mike's voice. He takes in a deep breath of air. "Charles graduated from high school and then college. He took a low paying but secure job, worked his way up the ladder, and eventually became a consultant. Then the company decided to outsource work overseas, and well, you can guess the rest. He lost his job." He clears his throat as he looks at the cigar. It seems lonely, just sitting there by itself. He wants to take another quick puff but delays taking action until later. "I got a hold of some of his medical records."

Mike grins and remains quiet.

"Starting when he was a kid and up until now he suffers from some sort of sleep disorder. He walks in his sleep but has no recollection of it happenin'. He's been temporarily hospitalized for depression, feelings of loneliness, and despair. Then he and Cassandra Lilia met. After a short engagement they got married." He takes another look at the cigar, longing for a final puff, feeling the sensation of the smoke fill his lungs and then letting the exhale fill the room. He refocuses. "That's it."

Silence slices through the conversation for a few seconds.

Mike says, "I've got something else that needs to be done. Find the right guys to do it and make it look like a suicide."

"Sure boss, anything you say. How soon do you want it done?"

"Right away."

"I'm listening, give me the details."

Ω Ω Ω Ω Ω

It is Monday morning. Charles is up and about early. He should be cheery about his first day of work, yet he wonders how he will deal with Denise when they meet.

Cass and Charles each stand in front of separate wash basins to get ready for work. There is a large mirror that extends the full length of the bathroom counter.

She washes her face as Charles shaves. Out of the corner of her eye, she sees his right hand clumsily jerk the razor that nicks his skin.

"Ouch." He sees from the mirror's image a small spot of blood ooze from the cut.

She puts down the wash cloth and turns towards him.

He notices her look by way of the mirror. "What?" His hand holding the razor shakes.

"Is something bothering you? You seem jittery."

He continues to look at her in the mirror. "Maybe just a little worked up about making the right impression on the first day. You know what they say about first impressions."

She does not buy his answer. "Sure, but, I have a feeling there is something else going on. You're more than

130

worked up, you're agitated." She takes a tissue out of a small package to dab the cut.

"Oh, this?" He points to the nick. "It's nothing. I must have put a new blade in the razor and forgot about it."

She presses the tissue more firmly against his skin. "You know you can tell me anything."

"Honey, you're making something out of nothing." He glances away from looking at her eyes. He takes in a deep breath and then slowly lets out some air. "I'm hoping to hear from Mike. He might call today and if I'm tied up in a meeting I won't be able to take his call." He doesn't think he has fooled her.

She's lived with him long enough to know when he is hiding something. Call it a sixth sense. Cass decides it best to let it go for now. She figures he will talk when the time is right, not now. She puts her arms around his neck. "I love you. Give me a big kiss."

They embrace for a short time.

She feels his body tighten up, and interprets it as a worried sign.

"And I love you," he says as he pulls away. "We should give a yell to Scarlet Rose. She's got morning classes."

Cass forces a weak smile. "I'll take care of her. You finish shaving. You don't want to be late either."

Ω Ω Ω Ω Ω

Charles stops by the receptionist desk. "Hi Jennie, I'm Charles Westfield. I start today. Do you remember me from last week?"

The perky woman smiles and then says, "Yes, Mr.

Westfield. Welcome. Your office is all set up for you. Do you know where it is?"

"Yes, thanks. Is that all?"

"Well, Mr. Jessup would like to talk with you before this morning's staff meeting. His office is just around the corner."

"Thanks."

"He hasn't yet arrived but I'll leave him a message that you're here. He should be here any minute."

"Fine, I'll just go to my office and settle in. Thanks."

"Yes, have a great day."

Charles walks towards his office. He feels his body tighten a little, worried about meeting with Denise. He hastens his pace a little hoping to pass her office just up ahead without having to take a peak in or say anything. He feels his heart pick up a beat. Now about two feet from her office, he struggles to keep his head straight ahead. However, the temptation to look to his right is much too strong. He glances towards her office. Then he stops. The office is empty. His breathing pauses, and then reboots. Relieved, he continues on.

"Hey, Charles. Welcome."

Charles turns to find a welcoming face. "Thanks, Mark, good to be here." He waits for the man to get closer.

"I'm so happy you've joined us. I can assure you it will not be dull."

"That's exactly what I'm hopeful for. Jennie says there's a staff meeting this morning. Is there anything I should be prepared for?"

"Not on your first day. Alan will probably give you a company welcome, and then tell us what's on the calendar for the week. The Monday morning meeting is the way to get everyone on the same page from the start. Then we have a Friday afternoon meeting to analyze what happened during the week and to get ready again for the following Monday. A few of the guys will report on things they've been tasked to look into."

"That seems straightforward enough."

Mark lowers his voice. "There is something you should be aware of, although we don't openly talk about it. It's just assumed."

Charles opens his eyes a wee bit wider. "What's that?"

"You know we're a startup company. Sometimes we hire the wrong type of person who doesn't really understand how fast the pace is. A lot of times it seems we're disorganized. And to be honest, sometimes we are. It's the sort of culture where you've got to pick up things quickly, adapt and adjust. We make decisions on limited information. There are few second chances. But I guess you know that. Right?"

"Yeah, but what are you really saying?"

"People come and go. There's no big announcement when someone leaves. That's just the way it is."

Charles steps closer. "So who left?"

Mark says flatly, "The Human Resources Director, Denise Cameon."

"Oh." It is all Charles can manage to say.

"She will certainly be missed by some of us guys. I mean … she was hot." Mark grins.

"Yeah." Charles swallows. "What were the circumstances?"

"Like I said before, people come and go. That's just how it is."

"Will she be replaced?"

"That's up to Alan. But I suspect he will want someone in that role. Why, do you know someone?"

Charles immediately thinks of his wife, but quickly decides to let the thought stay alone with him. "No." The one word answer is sufficient.

Mark says, "I don't either. Anyway, I've got to get ready for the meeting. I'll be reporting on our sales projections. See you in a while."

Charles sees Mark walk away, and then he steps towards his office.

It takes less than a minute for Charles to get to his office. He sits in a leather executive chair behind his desk and looks around the room thinking how to personalize the appearance. Then he opens a few drawers to see what's inside. He finds a few loose paperclips, a couple of hanging folders, and a stapler. Next he leans back in the chair to refocus on something else, the unexpected departure of Denise. He says to himself, "Maybe there's nothing to it. It is what it is." Something inside, however, tells him differently. He turns the chair around to look through a large window. His reflections are suddenly interrupted when he hears his name called out. He slightly jumps from the sound but when he turns around he sees Alan Jessup.

"Welcome, Charles. Good to have you join us." Alan steps into the office and extends his hand for a shake.

Charles stands to extend his hand. "Hi, Alan. Thanks. I'm happy to be here."

"Please, no need to stand. We're quite informal around here."

"Yes, of course." Charles sits down after shaking hands.

Alan continues. "We have a staff meeting today that you'll attend. Nothing for you to do other than a short introduction. Keep it real short. You'll get to know the team as you work with them, and they'll get to know you as well. We're pretty informal around here. First names are apt."

"Thanks. I bumped into Mark just a few seconds ago."

"He's our fisherman. I count on him quite heavily for sales to move this organization forward. That doesn't mean, of course, that I don't count on everyone else, like you."

Charles nods his head. "I understand what you mean. It takes a team effort." He pauses, and then thinks to ask a question.

Alan picks up on the hesitation from Charles. "What's up?"

Surprised that he gave away an inner thought, Charles feels his body heat up. His face turns red.

"I'm told I can read minds. I really can't but I know when someone is thinking about something they want to ask or get off their mind. What is it?"

"I was just wondering how you know Mike Aviara?"

"Who, that name is not familiar to me?"

"Oh, I thought he was the one who recommended me?"

"I don't know anything about that. We work with an

135

executive search firm. Maybe your guy knows someone in that firm. That's the job of our HR Director."

"Oh, I see." Charles wants to ask a follow up question. But before he can get it off his lips Alan gives him the answer.

"Did you interview with anyone from Bent and Brooks, the executive search firm?"

"Yes, and then with Denise, you and your staff."

"I don't see a problem. I'm not the HR pro but I guess that's how she did it. Anyway, it worked out well for you and us."

"Yeah, I guess it did."

"Speaking of our HR Director, Denise unexpectedly left us last week. I usually don't have all-employee meetings when people are hired and when they leave. I let the HR Director take care of that. But in this situation, I made an exception. Since the HR role touches everyone in the company, I didn't want employees wondering about her departure. I want them to focus on doing their work. So I told everyone the truth that Denise left us due to a personal matter. She said there was a family issue she had to take care of out of state. I told her I'd give her a paid leave but she decided against it. Now, I've got to find her replacement."

"Oh, I see." Charles is stuck on the same response.

"Now don't worry when things like that happen around here. Stuff happens outside of work that people need to deal with. I'll make sure her job is covered somehow. By the way, do you know a good HR Director?" Alan smiles.

"Ah, I'm sorry, no."

"Too bad. I'll get Bent and Brooks going on a

replacement this week. Anyway, I've got to prepare for this morning's meeting. Be prompt at 9 AM. We have a lot to cover." Alan stands and then walks towards the opened office door. Then he turns. "By the way, you'll need a laptop. Everyone has one. Take the one in Denise's old office. It's sitting on a small table. I'll have our IT guy, Paul, configure it for you today and load some important material that you'll need to get up to speed with."

"Got it. See you at 9."

Ω Ω Ω Ω Ω

The interrogation room is fifteen feet square. Black smudges on the white walls tip off that maintenance is overdue. Four gray metal chairs that surround a matching table rest on a black and white checkered linoleum floor. A ceiling light illuminates the space.

The sleeves of Detective Atra's white shirt are rolled up to just below the elbows. His blue tie has a noticeable coffee stain. He stands across the table where Mike Aviara sits in a chair.

Mike self-assuredly asks, "What's this all about?" His posture is erect and his stare is defiant. He folds his hands on top of the table, one over the other.

"Just a few questions. You know the routine. It'll be over before you know it." Detective Atra gives Mike a grin.

Mike questions Detective Atra, "Do you know what time it is?"

"I'm asking the questions, not you."

For a few seconds they stare at each other in silence.

Detective Atra continues. "Last time I checked it was four in the afternoon. So what! Have you got a date?"

Mike insubordinately asks, "What do you think?"

"What do I think? I didn't think you cared about what I thought."

"You're right, I don't."

"Then why are you asking?"

Mike unfolds his hands to form clenched fists. "OK, enough of this crap. What's up?"

Detective Atra asks, "Do you want to lawyer up? You have that right, but I think you know that."

"No, no. I don't want to bother him with some dumb ass crap." Mike grinds his teeth. "What's on your mind?"

Detective Atra shoves a photo across the table. "Do you recognize him?"

Mike takes a quick glance, "Never seen him." His upper body tenses.

Detective Atra grins. "You sure you've never seen him? You want to take another look just to be sure?"

"Like I said, I've never seen him." Mike pushes the photo away from him. It skims across the table. Then, he looks away.

"OK, what about this one? Ever seen him?" The Detective slides another photo Mike's way.

With the same amount of time as before, Mike quickly glances towards the photo. "No, never seem him either."

"And you're sure about this, never seen either guy."

"Absolutely," Mike says, "Neither guy." He shuffles his feet beneath the table.

"Well, maybe you can help me out. I'm a little confused. Do you think you might help me out?"

Mike turns his face away from the Detective and then angles back to face him. He lets out a puff of air to show his annoyance. "Sure if it will end this crap."

Detective Atra shoves a third photo Mike's way. "What about this one?"

This time Mike takes a long stare at the photo. Pictured with Mike are the two men from the previous two photos. Mike has his arm hung around one of the men. Everyone is smiling. Mike is stone-faced, and then he grins. "I look pretty good. Who are the others?"

"I know you know them," says Detective Atra. "Try harder."

Mike takes another glance at the photo and pushes it away. He looks up at the ceiling light and then says. "Oh yeah, I remember." He returns to look at Detective Atra. "I barely know them. It was a fluke that they were at the same place I was at for a few days of vacation. I don't even remember their names and I don't know what we even talked about."

"So you're saying to me you don't know their names or what their business was? Is that right?"

"Yeah, yeah, that's what I'm saying." Mike smirks.

"But you guys look awfully chummy. Come on Mike, you've got to remember something about them and why this picture was taken."

Mike shakes his heads sideways. "No, honest to God, I don't remember."

"Well, let me enlighten you about these two guys. The guy you're holding onto is Jimmy Tommasone and the other one is Billy Friguletto. They're mobsters. They're both part of the underworld. Know what I'm talking about?"

Mike shakes his head sideways. "No kidding, I didn't know that."

"Really?" Detective Atra asks.

"Really, honest to God."

"Do you want to know what else I think?"

"You're going to tell me anyway."

"I think you're part of their business."

"Aw no, not me. I know a lot of people, but hey, not these guys," Mike confidently says. "No, not these types of guys."

"I want to believe you, I really do, but Mike, this photo tells me a different story. You've got to help me here," Detective Atra presses.

"What can I say? I just met them by accident."

"Why the photo? I mean … why take a picture with two guys you barely knew? That doesn't make sense."

"Like I said I barely knew them."

"Have you seen them since the photo was taken?"

"When was it taken?"

"Are you telling me you don't know when the photo was taken?"

"Yeah, that's what I'm saying."

"But you said earlier that you remembered meeting these guys during your vacation." Atra stares and then continues. "See what I mean, I'm confused."

"Hey, I take a lot of vacations. I don't remember everything."

"So you're a vacation-kind-of-guy?"

"We all need time to relax, even you."

"OK, back to my question."

"What was that again?"

Atra tightens his lips. "To the best of your recollection, have you seen them since the photo was taken?"

Mike hesitates before answering. He is not sure if other pictures might be floating around that could implicate him with criminal activities. Yet he knows better than to admit any affiliation with crooks. "Like I said, I don't remember when the photo was taken." He pauses. "I'm just a little guy running a legitimate business. I have no idea why you think I would be involved in something that is against the law."

"Hey, Mike, I never said you've done anything illegal. All I've asked here is if you know when the photo was taken and if you know these guys."

Mike believes saying anything more might backfire, so he repeats his previous statements. He lowers his voice, and leans forward. "I just met them by accident. That's it."

"Anything else you want to say?"

"No, I think that's it."

"OK, Mike. Thanks for coming down. If you think of anything after you leave, give me a call." Detective Atra stares at Mike. "You can now go."

His voice sounds relieved, "Is that it?"

"What, you want to hang around?"

"No."

"That's it. You can go."

Mike leaves with an unofficial warning hanging over him that he could be called back into questioning again.

Ω Ω Ω Ω Ω

Shortly after Mike leaves Detective Atra, Detective Kline enters the room.

Detective Atra asks, "What do you think?"

Detective Kline says, "He's pretty confident, but I saw him tense up a few times."

"Yeah, I picked up on it. But I was really hoping to rattle him enough to get him to lose his temper."

Detective Kline adds, "This is not the first time he's been questioned. He's had enough experience being interrogated."

"Practice makes perfect."

"We know Aviara is involved in the shakedown of strip clubs."

"And we know that Tommasone and Friguletto are behind it."

Detective Kline pauses, looks away for a second and faces his partner again. "Yeah, but we've got to prove it."

"The people who are being intimidated are afraid to come forward. That's why no one is talking. They think everything is hunky-dory just the way it is. But what they don't realize is their protection payments will go up and up."

Detective Kline nods his head. "Somebody has to come forward one of these days."

"But only when the pain is so much they can't stand it."

"I hear you." Detective Kline shakes his head.

Detective Atra says, "I'm going to keep close tabs on Aviara. He's going to mess up and I want to be the first one in his face. He's either deep into crime activities or else just a little guy who is sucked into the thrill of being with men he better not mess with."

ΩΩΩΩ

Later that evening after dinner, Scarlet Rose says to her parents, "I'm going to Wanda's house to study."

Cass reminds her daughter, "Be sure to be home by nine."

"Yes I remember." She rolls her eyes and then leaves the house.

Charles says, "Alan wants me to look over a few things that have been loaded on the laptop I brought home. I'll be upstairs."

Cass asks, "When have you gotten to be computer savvy?"

"The IT guy showed me a few things, real basic stuff like how to open, save, and delete files. Nothing too fancy."

"Yeah those are the basics." She smiles. "But remember what you promised."

"I remember. I said I would not take work home. This is an exception."

"I'm going to keep you to your promise. You know I will."

"Of course, but when the boss asks for something, I think it's best to do it. I shouldn't be more than an hour. I promise."

"OK, I'm timing you."

Charles smiles as he steps up the stairs to get settled.

He pushes a small side button that activates the laptop. In less than ten seconds the screen's laptop displays the company's logo and a welcome message. His eyes scan icons situated at the left margin. He remembers what Paul, the IT guy, told him what to look for. He spots it.

He clicks on MISSION that takes him to five pages of the company's Mission, Purpose, Strategic Plan, and Core Values. He reads the material carefully. "I'm impressed," he thinks. "This is quite remarkable."

Next, he clicks on ADMINISTRATION. Immediately the page gives him a template to create his Department's Mission, Purpose, Strategic Plan, and Core Values. "This is going to take some time, but what a great idea to have each Department create their own set of principles that align with each other Department and then to the Company's set of principles." He drops his fingers from the keyboard to think about a few things. Then he takes out a note pad to scribble a few ideas. He continues for another thirty minutes or so. "This is a good start," he thinks. He checks his watch and notices that he is about out of time. He doesn't want to disappoint Cass.

Charles is about to give a yell to Cass to let her know he is coming when he catches sight of something else. His eyes widen from inquisitiveness. The Recycle Bin contains previously deleted files. Curious, he clicks on the Recycle Bin icon. There are fifteen files still in the Bin. Charles wonders whether to empty them or wait to ask Alan which ones are important. About to turn off the laptop he notices one file in particular, a video. It is titled GOTYA. He wonders what it could be. He remembers Paul cautioning him about opening unknown files, but in this case he figures there is no harm since it is already loaded on the computer. He clicks on the file. In less than ten seconds the screen changes to something quite familiar. He recognizes his and Denise's voice and then their faces. Within a short time he sees and hears it all. His jaw drops and his eyes widen more than they ever have before. He cannot believe it. His heart starts to accelerate and he feels clammy all over. He knows how the video will end, yet, he cannot find it in him to stop it.

Cass yells out. "What's going on up there? Are you watching a movie?"

The sound of her voice startles him. He quickly stops the video. "I don't believe this!"

"If you're watching a movie, I'm coming up to join you."

"Oh, no. I'm coming down." His fingers tremble while various ambiguous thoughts bump into each other. He blinks a few times to refocus. He deletes the file and then empties all the contents within the Recycle Bin. Finally, he shuts down the laptop. For the next several seconds he stares at a black screen. His mind for the time being is void of what next to do. His body is frozen in place.

"Honey, have you forgotten me?"

Her voice takes him out of the self-imposed trance. "No, no. I'm on my way." He firmly grabs the laptop as if it is his only possession in the world, and then slowly walks down the stairs to join his wife.

She makes a face that is far from being a smile, more of a frown. "What's up? You look as if you've seen a ghost."

The laptop is now securely clenched in both hands. White knuckles are apparent. At first he does not hear her words.

"What's the matter? You look frightened." She touches the right side of the couch. "Come here by my side."

Charles slowly walks her way. The laptop is still safe in his hands.

"I opened a bottle of Port. Here, take a glass." Her

voice is calm but she wonders why he looks upset. "You've got to say something."

He sits alongside Cass. The laptop is now pressed closely against his chest. He takes in a deep breath of air and then slowly exhales. Finally, he pulls out of the haze, yet he is not able to find the strength to look at her face to face. "I have something to tell you."

She touches his arm and then lightly squeezes. "You can tell me anything, you know that." Cass looks bewildered.

"Something happened at the office that I am not proud of, something terrible." He feels a little dizzy.

Cass holds her breath for a second and then exhales. She realizes something is really troubling him. "Go on, I'm listening."

Charles waits a few seconds before he continues. He keeps his looks away from her. "It was like a movie, strange and surreal."

Cass is confused so she remains quiet to let her husband find a way to get out his thoughts.

Slowly Charles regains sufficient alertness to tell a partially fabricated story. He slowly turns his head to face her. "I told you about the HR Director, didn't I?"

Cass isn't sure what he means. She sees uneasiness in his eyes. "I'm not sure. Talk to me."

"Alan told me this morning that she had unexpectedly resigned last week. I guess it was soon after meeting with me to complete the new hire paperwork." He pauses to find the right words.

"Oh, why did she quit?"

"Family reasons, I think that's what he told me, must

have been serious." He begins to feel more comfortable in telling the story.

"So, what's the problem? I don't understand."

Charles takes in a deep breath and then slowly breathes out. He angles his eyes downward. "I think she was kinky."

Cass frowns. "You mean ... a voyeur?"

"Yeah, something like that."

"How do you know?"

He clears his throat. His head is still turned downward, away from her. "I just saw a video of her."

"While you were upstairs?" Cass stares at Charles for a long time before he answers.

He senses her stare so he keeps his face turned away. In a meek sounding voice he finally replies, "Yes."

She can't believe her ears. Cass opens her eyes wider than normal. "What were you doing, surfing the Internet?"

Charles feels as if he just swallowed a piece of an apple that is stuck in his throat. He coughs a few times and then with a little more assertiveness in his voice he replies. "No, nothing like that." He shakes his head.

"Did it have something to do with the sound I heard while you were upstairs?"

He pauses and clears his throat again, "Yes it did."

"So it must have been a video you were watching upstairs. Is that it?"

Charles looks at his wife, surprised. His face is chalk colored white. "How did you know?"

"Simple deduction."

"Oh." He gazes away.

"Look at me!"

Slowly he turns to face her but quickly his eyes angle downwards.

"Please look at me."

He lifts his head to face her.

"What was on the video?"

He forces to keep looking toward her, but at the same time trying to shield some truth. "She was having sex with a man."

"You're kidding me?"

He moves his head sideways, "No, it was definitely she and a man."

"Do you recognize the man she was with?"

He clears his throat. "No, no one I met from the office today."

"So she was having sex with a man you don't know. Is that it?"

"That's right. I've never seen him before."

"When did it happen?"

"Well, I think it was videoed in her office at one time. I don't know when."

Cass gains more interest in the story. "Do you think either one knew they were being filmed?"

"Yes."

"Who, was it him or her?"

"I think it was her. I don't think the guy knew what was going on."

"How do you know that?"

"I don't know, I'm just guessing."

"Was it like she was in control and he was simply reacting to her?"

"Come to think of it, yes, I think that's how it was."

"An example of a woman in control and in charge. That's not unusual, especially these days."

He shrugs his shoulders.

Cass continues. "So she was doing her thing, the way she wanted it done."

Charles is not sure if it is his turn to talk so he keeps quiet.

Cass continues. "What's the big deal? I mean, why are you so upset about this?"

Charles pulls himself together. "Come on. I'm the new guy who's trying to figure out the culture of the company. Now I've come across a video of the former HR Director having sex with a man in her office. If you were in my shoes wouldn't you be upset, even just a little?"

Cass says, "I see your point. Maybe I'm overreacting."

"More like minimizing it."

"OK, I'm with you on that."

He settles down a bit. "Maybe each of us is simply reacting differently."

"But we both agree she's probably a voyeur, and gets off on seeing herself dominate a man through sex."

"Yeah, that's right. There are those types of people around." Charles wants the conversation to stop, but he can't figure out how to do it.

"Why was the video on your laptop? I don't get that at all." Then Cass puts her hands to her mouth. "Are you trying to tell me who the man is?"

Charles looks towards Cass. He fears she's figured out it was him. "No. It wasn't me. I told you I didn't recognize the man." He pauses and looks away to collect his thoughts. Then he refocuses on his wife. "The company gave me her laptop. I guess she didn't delete the video. I don't think anyone other than her knew the video was still there."

She hesitates for a short time to catch her breath. Then she lets out a breath of air. "Of course, what was I thinking?" She grabs hold of his arm.

His arm stiffens as he feels her firm grip.

She feels his reaction so she lessens her hold. "You can put the laptop down."

He looks surprised to see the laptop still in his grasp. "Oh, I forgot I was holding it. Yeah." He sets the laptop on the side opposite to where Cass sits.

"Is the video still there?" Cass nods her head towards the laptop.

"Why do you want to know that?"

"I'd like to see it." Her voice is suddenly upbeat.

Charles is flabbergasted. "You want to watch the video?"

"Sure, why not. You saw it, now it's my turn."

Charles stops dead in thoughts. He can't let her see him and Denise.

She rescues him in the nick of time. She teases Charles. "Maybe there is something we can learn, you know, to spice up our sex."

Taken aback with her comment, Charles does not pick up on the kidding."Our sex isn't so bad. Come on."

"I'm joking."

He does not know what to say so he remains quiet.

She fills in the silence. "Oh, come on honey. Let me just have a little peek." She snuggles close to him, and then blows softly into his ear. "Just a little."

He hangs back from answering, so she moves ahead.

"Just to sneak a quick look, that's all." She massages his neck.

"I deleted the video. It's gone."

She straightens her posture, and her voice changes to sounding aloof. "Too bad, it would have been interesting to see just the same." She stares at the laptop a short distance away and then continues. "Do you think anybody in the company knew of her sexual tendencies?"

Relieved that the conversation has shifted, he answers, "Good question, but I don't know. However, I wonder now if her unexpected departure had anything to do with the video."

"Why would you make that connection?"

Charles shrugs his shoulders, "I don't know. The idea just popped into my head."

"Was she attractive?"

Charles thinks twice before answering. He cocks his head to the side. "I guess some people might think so. I thought she was average looking." He waits a few seconds and continues. "But not close to being as beautiful as you." He smiles and feels his body drain of tension.

"Perfect answer." She pulls his face close to her and firmly presses her lips against his. They stay embraced for a while.

He flip-flops about whether to tell her the real story. In the end, at least for now, he decides to keep the falsehood alive.

Cass grabs both wine glasses. "Here, take this glass of Port. We need to toast to continued health and happiness."

CHAPTER 5

It is three days later. Mike has not returned Charles' phone call. He wonders what's up, so, inside his office he places a follow up call from his cell phone. After hearing the outgoing message, he says, "Hey, Mike. This is Charles Westfield. I left a message a few days ago about my daughter, Scarlet Rose. Can you give me a call as soon as possible? Thanks." He disconnects, holds the cell phone in his hand for a short time, and continues to wonder why Mike seems to be unavailable. Then a sudden but familiar voice interrupts his inner thoughts.

"Charles."

He turns to the sound of his name. "Alan, what's up?"

"I want to go over your recommendations for your Department's Mission, Purpose, Strategic Plan, and Core Values. Come on over to my office."

"Sure."

The meeting between Alan and Charles lasts close to an hour.

Alan says, "I like it. I think if you share this with the other Department Heads you'll start to fine-tune the information. Then, we'll put everything together to make sure that all Departments support one another and support the overall Company. OK?"

Charles lets his body slouch for a second and then he straightens up. Something is on his mind. He clears his throat. "Alan, something has been bothering me and I've got to get this off my chest."

Alan nods his head just enough to indicate it is OK for Charles to continue.

Charles looks away to bring together enough strength to go on. Slowly he faces Alan. "It's about Denise Cameon."

Straight-faced, Alan asks, "I've already told the staff that the search firm is looking for her replacement."

"Yes, I know that. It's something else." Charles feels a little dizzy so he takes in a breath of air through his nose and gradually lets the air escape through the same passage way.

"Then what is it?" Alan continues. "I don't understand."

"It's about her and me."

Alan frowns. "Go on." He leans back in his chair.

He takes in another deep breath and then gives out a heave-ho of air through his nose. "She seduced me." All of a sudden Charles feels relief.

Alan grins. "She did what?" He tilts his head to the side.

Charles, now more comfortable that the secret is out, continues. "She got me to have sex with her."

Alan lets out a laugh.

Charles is taken aback. His eyes widen, flabbergasted. He manages to say, "Really, she did."

"I'm sorry to have laughed, but honestly, why are you telling me this?"

"She videoed the entire thing on her laptop." He smacks his lips and then picks up where he left off. "This has never happened to me. I mean … never."

"Charles, I' m really not interested in what employees do on their own time, as long as it doesn't adversely impact the company. What you do away from this office on your personal time is your business, not mine. So, if this pertains to the company, I'm interested. If it is something personal I don't want to know."

"It happened in her office, between Denise and me."

Alan doesn't blink. He props his elbows on the arms of his chair and touches the tips of the fingers from both hands to each other that results in a triangular appearance. Calmly he says, "Go on."

Charles' voice returns to a noticeable quiver as he continues. "In the evening, after hours, when no one was around. It happened in her office after I completed all my new hire paperwork. I think it was Thursday or maybe Wednesday before I started work on Monday." He pauses and then repeats, "Nobody was here at the time, just us two. I'm sure of it, just me and her."

Alan keeps silent for a short time. He has never heard of anything like this happening in all his years of work. "So, you and her had sex in her office one evening, is that what you're telling me?"

"Yes, that's what I'm saying." Charles feels as if his insides are erupting.

Alan still wonders if Charles is telling him the truth. Yet, he keeps quiet to let Charles resume.

Charles starts out speaking calmly. "We finished all

the paperwork to get me into the payroll and HR systems. Then, she leaned over to ask if she could do anything else. I figured she meant, you know, with work. But no, she meant something different." He pauses for a second.

Alan drops his hands onto the desk, palms downward. "Why are you telling me these details?"

Charles stares at Alan. "I thought you'd want to know."

"I am not interested in hearing any of the details with regards to the physical contact between you and her, but you said she videoed it entirely."

"Yes, yes. I didn't know it at the time, but when you gave me her laptop, I found the video in the Recycle Bin." His voice rises, "I saw it! It was all there!"

Alan glances away. A grin creases his face and then he looks back at Charles. "You do know this is a mind-boggling story."

Charles agrees, "Yes I do, but it's the truth. Why would I say it if it wasn't true?"

"I'm not saying it is or is not true. All I'm saying is that it is amazing what happened." He pauses. "Why would she come on to you like that? He shifts his body to the side and crosses his legs.

"I have no idea, none whatsoever."

"Is the video still on the laptop?

Charles quickly answers. "I deleted it. It's gone. I couldn't stomach to keep it."

Alan shakes his head. "No, nothing is ever deleted from a computer." He pauses. "I want to see the video. I'll get Paul to recover it and we'll see it together."

Charles shakes his head sideways. "No." He stares at Alan in silence and then carries on. "Why, don't you believe me? Do you think I'd make up something like this?"

"Charles, I don't know what to believe, but first things first." He straightens in the chair and points his right index finger at Charles. "If something like this happened in my office, then I want to see it. This office is not a place for sexual affairs. It's pretty simple to understand." He takes in a deep breath and lowers his hand. "In fact, if what you're saying is true, I could fire you. If Denise were still here I could fire her as well." Without hesitation, he reaches for a phone on his desk to dial an interoffice number. "Hey, Paul, come on down to my office. I need you to do something." He turns to Charles, "Go get your laptop and bring it here. It'll be just between you and me, alone, no one else, I promise. I do have to see the video."

Charles remains frozen in place for a short time, and then stands. "You're going to see that I've told you the truth. Will you still fire me in spite of her being the aggressor?"

"Probably not. I realize you didn't have to come forward to tell me. Let's take one step at a time. Now, please get the laptop."

Charles walks in a robot like way to retrieve the laptop. On his way he passes Paul in the hallway.

Paul casually says, "Hey, what's up?"

Charles forces a grin that does not fool anyone. He stays headed towards his office.

Now inside his own office, he tries to stare down the laptop. Obviously, it does not work but Charles feels a little better just trying to make it disappear. He picks up the black machine and then makes his way back to Alan's office.

By the time Charles returns to Alan's office, Paul is seated in a chair next to Alan who has repositioned himself from behind his desk. An empty third chair is available around the circular table for Charles to take.

Alan motions to Charles. "Give Paul the laptop." Then he turns to Paul. "There is a video that was deleted a few days ago. All I want you to do is to retrieve it, but not open it."

Paul shrugs his shoulders. "That's it?"

"That's all there is. Charles and I need to take a look at it."

"Can I ask what's on the video?"

"No," Alan flatly answers.

Paul raises his eyebrows. "OK. Does the video have a file name?"

Alan looks at Charles for a response, but when he sees Charles shrugs his shoulders, he says, "I'm sure it does, but I don't know it. Just look for any video that was deleted a few days ago or less. I can't imagine there are that many."

"OK, let's see what I can find." Paul opens the laptop and within seconds begins a search process to identify deleted files. It takes less than three minutes. He smiles. "Simple." He smiles. "There's only one deleted video so it wasn't difficult to find. I'll restore it to the desktop and it should be good as new." He presses a few more keys and then says. "OK, here it is." He hands over the laptop to Alan. "Interesting title." He grins and then finishes, "Is there anything else I can do?"

"That should do it. Thanks. Charles and I need to take a look."

Paul picks up the signal to leave the office. He goes away without comment.

"OK, Charles, let's see what we have here." Alan opens the video as Charles remains seated across the table. "This first part shows her giving you instructions to complete the paperwork." His eyes are glued on the laptop screen. "Pretty standard."

Charles closes his eyes to blank out the entire event. He hears his own breathing.

Other than the muted sound heard from the laptop's speakers, it is otherwise silent in the room for several minutes. Then all of a sudden things change.

"Ah." Alan's expression turns to surprise. "I see what you mean." His eyes are stuck to the screen. He shakes his head sideways but otherwise, keeps silent.

Charles knows exactly what Alan sees. He looks away for a short time and then back towards his boss.

The video ends, the screen is blank, Alan remains motionless and speechless. A few seconds pass before he looks at Charles to say, "She is one hell of a woman." Then he lets out a nervous laugh. "I still don't understand why this happened. What was her motive for seducing you?" He stops talking to try to process the situation. "It was evident you did not invite this, it was all her doing." There is another temporary halt. "And then she unexpectedly resigned." He looks away and then back to Charles. "I don't know what to make of it. Do you?" He taps his lips with his right index finger.

Charles lets out a breath of air. He tries to settle down, but that proves difficult. His voice quivers. "I-I have no idea."

"Did you know her before you joined us? I mean

… could there be some history between you and her, or between someone from your family and her, maybe even a friend, a neighbor, anyone?"

"No, this is a total shock to me. I met her only because of the job interview." Charles feels his body calm down a little, thankful that his boss seems to be on his side.

"Have you told anyone about this?"

Charles lies, "No one other than you knows." He figures Joe will keep the secret under wraps.

"So this means your wife as well."

"I was very close to telling her the other night when I found the video, as I was reviewing the company's mission statement and goals, but I backed out the last second."

"Good decision." Alan clears his throat. "Can I offer you some advice?"

Charles leans forward, "Certainly, what is it?"

"Don't tell anyone, I mean … no one."

"Really?"

"Not even your priest, if you have one."

"Why?" He takes a deep swallow. "I'm feeling this heavy burden on my shoulders."

"You might have to carry the burden for the rest of your life, but that's your personal choice. If I were you, I'd keep it a secret."

"I feel crappy."

"That might be the price you'll have to pay. That's just how it is."

"I don't like it."

"Do what you need to do, but listen to me first. I'm not an alarmist, but a realist. One thing I've learned with other startup companies I've founded is to plan for worse case scenarios in case of disasters. I'd classified this video as a disaster. You do not want this video to get in the wrong hands, meaning, someone who wants to blackmail you to keep it hidden. You might think that Denise was simply having a cheap thrill at your expense, and maybe she was. But there might be more to it. So I'd consider this situation in need of a disaster plan. I think you should make a copy of the video for yourself and keep it locked up in a safe deposit box or someplace else where no one can ever find it, except you. If this topic ever comes up again you'll have evidence. I'm a believer in limiting access to important information, and this video is important information." Alan pauses. He sees Charles' anxious eyes and then he continues. "And I'm going to do you a favor, a big favor. I am willing to totally destroy the hard drive on this laptop so that nothing can be recovered. I'll do it in front of you. I could discipline you in some way for participating in this activity, but the video clearly shows me you are the victim in this case."

"I-I appreciate this."

"Sure." He pauses. "I think you're a stand-up guy, but you got yourself unknowingly into this mess. I don't want to see it get out of hand and I don't want you to get harmed. I know you're worried, I can see it in your eyes and hear it in your voice."

"Should I go to the police?"

"And what would you say to them, that you've got a video of you and a woman having sex? Come on. No, as I said before, keep this between you and me. You do trust me, don't you?"

Charles is quick to respond, "Definitely, yes. I trust you."

"I don't know what else to say or do. You have to do

whatever is best for you. That's a personal choice, I know. But don't do something emotionally based. Think it out first, logically. OK?"

Charles extends his hand towards Alan to shake on it. "Yes yes, you're making a lot of sense. Thanks for your understanding and belief in me."

"Sure, not a problem. I hope you'd protect my back if I ever needed it."

"I guarantee I would."

"Now, let me make a copy of the video to put on a DVD, and then remove the hard drive from the computer and destroy it. I know how to do both. I'll do it right now in front of you. Then I'll have a replacement hard drive installed in the laptop." He pauses. "OK?"

"Yes."

Ω Ω Ω Ω Ω

The room is dimly lit, just enough overhead lights to check out each other and the cards in their hands. Behind, in a corner, are opened liquor bottles; scotch, rye, gin, and bourbon. A few empty glasses are nearby but most are on top of the poker table next to each player. On another table is a variety of food; antipasto, sausage with potatoes, eggplant, and salami-ham-tomato-provolone sandwiches. The last table holds the desserts of orange biscotti, marsala biscotti, and hazelnut cookies along with black coffee and sugar.

Vince puffs on a half-smoked cigar but manages to say, "I'm a compulsive gambler. I love it and can't get enough of it."

Across from Vince is Ronnie. He shuffles in one hand

his last remaining chips. "What the hell am I doin' here?" He stares at the pot of chips in the middle of the table. "I never win."

Mike takes in a deep breath of air, and then a sip of scotch. "You're here because you want to be here. Don't crap on yourself."

Ronnie answers. "You wanna know somethin', Mike? I don't care what you think. Fuck off."

Mike grins. He knows Ronnie is close to bailing out of the game.

Ritchie keeps quiet for the time being. He is trying to size up the game.

Mike asks, "Ritchie, you're quiet. What gives? You don't want to talk with us? Are you too good to talk with us?"

Vince says, "Mike, let it go. Let's get back to the game."

Ritchie twists a blue ring on his pinky finger. He looks up at Mike who wears a white dress shirt opened at the collar. "Yeah Mike, let's get back to the game."

Mike changes the topic. "Ronnie, how's your squeeze. Is she doing you OK?"

Ronnie places his cards on the table. He ignores Mike's comment. "I gotta take a piss. Nobody look at my hand." He finishes off the last of the bourbon in his glass with one swallow and then slams the empty glass on top of the poker table.

Mike says, "You're not a good gambler. You should get out; do something you can do better than losing money."

"I'm not a good gambler?" Ronnie looks at Mike. "Who the fuck are you to tell me what I'm good at and what I'm not good at?" He pulls out a gun. "You wanna know what I'm good at? Huh?" He points the gun directly at Mike.

Mike remains calm. "OK, Ronnie. I'll make you a deal."

Ronnie looks surprised and then glances around at the other men who remain quiet. Finally he returns to look at Mike. "What's that, what deal do you have for me?"

"I promise not to screw your squeeze anymore if you put the gun away." Mike grins.

"All right, all right." Vince interrupts. He looks at Ronnie, "Put the gun away and take your piss." Then he looks at Mike, "One of these days your luck is gonna run out."

"Like what?" Mike looks around at the hoodlums. "Nobody can do anything to me." He takes a sip of scotch.

Ritchie says, "They can plant stuff on you."

Mike answers, "Done before, no big deal."

Ritchie says, "They can do what they did to Sal." He glances around the table. "Cut his head, feet, and hands off."

Mikes replies, "Sal was stupid. He should have never gone alone to meet them. I'm not stupid."

Vince says, "They can kill you anytime and anyplace."

As Ronnie walks away to take care of business, he adds his two cents, "Couldn't happen to a nicer guy."

Vince gets up from the poker table to walk to the desert table to grab one orange and one marsala biscotti.

Mike and Ritchie stay put at the table.

A few minutes later the four men are back at the

round poker table as if the previous conservation was unimportant.

Vince asks, "OK, let's get back to playin' poker. How many?"

Ritchie says, "Two."

Ronnie says, "Three."

Mike says, "One."

Vince says, "Dealer takes one."

Silence slices through the room for a minute. Then Vince says, "Ritchie, your call."

"I'm out." He turns his cards face down on the table. "Fuck this."

Vince says, "Ronnie, it's yours."

"Two hundred."

"Mike, it's up to you now."

"Up another hundred."

Vince says, "Christ."

Mike says, "OK Vince, it's your turn."

"Yours and three more."

Ronnie turns his cards over. "Cards are too cold. I'm out."

"Looks like it's you and me," Mike says. He peeks at his cards again, solemn face. "You probably got a full house. Is that it Vince, you got a full house?"

"You callin', raisin' or gettin' out?" Vince smiles broadly. "There's only way to find out."

"I call. Show me your hand?"

Vince lays his cards face up for everyone to see.

"Fuck it, a full house! I knew it!" Mike tosses his cards face down.

"Thank you," Vince says as he grabs the chips from the center of the round poker table. "Who's in?"

"Too rich for me," Ritchie says.

Vince looks at Mike, "How you feelin'? Ready to get your money back?"

Before Mike answers, Ronnie says, "I'm out."

Mike remains silent.

Vince keeps his stare towards Mike, "You're not peeved, are you? It's nothin' personal."

Mike finally answers, "I know, it's only business." He pauses, "Can you spot me a thou?"

"Gee Mike, I wish I could." Vince smirks as he nods his head sideways.

"Why, don't you think I'll pay you back?"

"It's like this, Mike. Business is business, and I don't think you're a good investment. No hard feelings. Like we said, it's only business. Know what I mean?"

Ω Ω Ω Ω Ω

A renter in Manor Arms Apartments, a large apartment complex, stops by the apartment manager's office. She is concerned. "Marge, papers and stuff are piling up outside of apartment 121. It's not like her to let that happen. I've knocked on her door a few times during the last few days but no one answers. I just thought you'd like to know. It seems weird."

"Thanks Jean, I'll look into it." Marge takes in a deep breath of air, shakes her head, and continues filling out an end-of-the month reconciliation form she has to submit to her boss by tomorrow. It takes her another ten minutes to complete the project before she walks towards apartment number 121.

On the way to the apartment she checks the assigned

parking space for apartment 121. She notices the renter's car still in place. "That's strange." She moves on.

Marge knocks on the door of apartment number 121. "Miss Cameon, are you in?" She listens but there is no answer. She glances down at her feet to check out the accumulated papers. She knocks again, and then reaches for a master key. "Miss Cameon, are you in?" After another no-response, Marge unlocks the door. "I'm coming in." She slowly opens the door, steps one foot inside and looks around. The apartment is neat and tidy but the air smells stale. "Anybody here?" She takes one more step inside, stops, and looks around again. Nothing seems to be out of order. She proceeds into the kitchen to find dishes and utensils in the sink. Then she moves to the bedroom to find everything in place. She shrugs her shoulders and leaves the apartment.

Back in her small office, Marge is not sure what next to do.

Ω Ω Ω Ω Ω

Later in the evening, Charles and Cass watch the late night news on television.

The television anchor says, "This is a late breaking story. A woman in her late twenties or early thirties was found dead a few hours ago in the desert. Our reports indicate her body was slightly decomposed signifying she died several days ago, but we can't we sure of that. Her name is unknown and the cause of her death remains unknown as well. We'll report any update as soon as we receive more information. To repeat, an unknown woman in her late twenties or early thirties was found dead in the desert just a few hours ago."

Cass turns to Charles, "So sad. I wonder if she had family."

Charles partially hears her, his mind is still processing the meeting with Alan earlier in the day. "Yeah."

Ω Ω Ω Ω Ω

Sitting alone in her apartment, Marge takes another sip of beer and then a long drag from a cigarette. She stares at a small television set, partially listening to the late night news before going to bed. Her eyes slowly widen as she hears the story of the dead female found in the desert. Unhurriedly, she rests the half glass of beer on a nearby table. The cigarette still clings to her lips as she remains quiet. She wonders about something but quickly shrugs it off. "No way, can't be her." She leans over to grab the glass of beer for another swallow but her hand begins to shake a little and her eyes widen bit by bit. She decides to make a phone call to the police.

Ω Ω Ω Ω Ω

Police arrive at Manor Arms Apartments a little after eleven that evening.

Marge stands outside the door of her apartment. She takes a final drag on a cigarette and then stuffs it out in an ashtray in her hand. She spots two police officers walk her way. "Over here." She waves their way.

Officer Dini asks Marge, "Are you the one who made the call?"

"Yes, that's me. I'm Marge Reilly. I'm the on-site manager of Manor Arms."

Officer O'Connor asks Marge, "You called in saying you believe the renter of one of your apartments is the same person who was recently found dead in the desert?"

Marge is shaken and her voice is rough sounding from too many beers and cigarettes. She manages to get out a single word. "Yes."

Officer Dini follows up, "Why do you suspect this?"

Marge coughs enough to make her throat feel rawer than it is. "She's always picks up her papers and I usually see her around the complex. Another renter noticed papers piling up in front of her place. She even knocked on her door several times but no one answered. It's just too strange. This is a safe place, and people look after one another around here. I guess I want to be safe than sorry." Marge coughs again.

Officer Dini says, "We'll want to talk with the other renter."

Marge answers, "Yes, of course."

Officer O'Connor asks, "Can you let us into the apartment?"

"Yes sir, this way." She moves towards the apartment. "I've already been inside the apartment, but I didn't touch anything. At least I don't remember touching anything. Everything inside seemed to be neat."

Officer Dini says, "Please stay outside until we take a look."

Marge steps aside to let the two police officers enter the apartment. She looks at the crushed cigarette butt in the ashtray. She longs for another one. Marge waits a long fifteen minutes before the police officers come back.

"I've called in for detectives. They should be here shortly," says Officer Dini.

Ω Ω Ω Ω Ω

Twenty minutes later two detectives arrive on scene. They talk with the two police officers to get updated, and then the two police officers leave the scene.

Detective Briley approaches Marge. "I know you've already told the police officers but would you tell us what happened here?"

"Yes, yes, of course," Marge answers.

While Marge repeats to Detective Briley the same information previously given to Police Officers Dini and O'Connor, Detective Cardinale enters the apartment.

Fifteen minutes pass before Detective Cardinale comes out of the apartment. "Yeah, there doesn't seem to be any signs of a struggle." Then she shows Marge a photo she found inside. "Is this her, the renter?"

Marge nods her head, "Yes, that's her, such a beautiful woman."

"There's a dog by her side. Did she have the dog here?" asks Detective Briley.

Marge nods her head sideways. "No. We don't allow pets."

Detective Cardinale says, "We're going to take this photo and match it as best we can to the deceased person's face."

Then Detective Briley asks, "Do you know if she had any tattoos, body piercings, or other external body markings?"

Marge thinks for a short time. "No, but honestly, I

really don't remember. I mean … I never really noticed anything. I'm sorry."

Detective Briley replies, "That's fine. We'll be sending a photographer to document the interior. We don't want anyone else to enter the apartment."

Marge understands. "Yes." She pauses and then adds, "I've got to tell the owner of the complex what's happened."

Detective Cardinale nods her head, "Of course. That's not a problem. Here, take my card should he want to talk with us."

Marge says, "She."

Detective Cardinale asks, "Excuse me?"

Marge clarifies, "It is a she who owns the complex. Shirley Livingstein."

Detective Cardinale replies, "Yes, tell her to call us if she wants."

"She won't be happy," Marge says.

"Why's that?" Detective Briley frowns.

"She'll want to rent the apartment quickly."

"Well that might be a problem," answers Detective Briley.

Marge continues, "Yeah, I understand, but who will want to rent this apartment when they find out that the former renter was the dead person found in the desert."

Detective Briley replies, "Yes, I see what you mean. But we don't know if they are the same person."

"She won't be happy," Marge softly says. "Shirley won't be happy."

Ω Ω Ω Ω Ω

Two days later Alan Jessup receives a surprise visitor at his office. He stands alongside Jennie at the receptionist desk as Detective Cardinale walks in.

"Hello, can I speak with Mr. Alan Jessup?"

"Who should I say is asking?" Jennie is polite.

"I'm Detective Cardinale."

Alan interrupts. "I'm Alan Jessup. Can you tell me what this is about?"

"Mr. Jessup, I'm Detective Cardinale. I hope you can help me with a current investigation." She shows him her Detective Badge. "Can you confirm that Denise Cameon worked for you at one time?"

"Yes, she was our Human Resources Director, but what is this about?"

She shows Alan the photo of Denise with her dog that was taken from the deceased's apartment. "Is this her?"

It takes Alan a short second to recognize the woman in the photo. "Yes it is. What's happened?"

"Maybe we should go somewhere we can talk privately."

Alan looks at Jennie who intently listens into the conversation.

"Yes, I see what you mean. Follow me into my office." He turns and then says to Jennie, "Hold all my calls. I don't want any interruptions."

"Yes, Mr. Jessup."

Now inside his office, Alan says, "Please, take a seat. What is this about?"

"How long did Ms. Cameon work for you?"

"Something like two months, but I can pull out her records to be exact. What's this about?"

"What was her capacity with your company?"

"She was our Human Resources Director. Is she is in some sort of trouble?"

"Do you know where she is now?"

"She unexpectedly left us a few days ago. She said it was a family emergency out of state. I didn't ask anything further. What's this about?"

"Did she leave any forwarding address?"

"No."

"And you are positive this is her in this photo?" Cardinale shows him the photo again.

Alan looks at it one more time to make sure, and then he angles his face towards her. "Yes, this is her. I'm positive. What's this about?"

"I'm sorry to say she was found dead in the desert a few days ago. I'm investigating her death." Unblinkingly, Cardinale looks straight into his eyes.

"My God!" Alan is authentically shocked. His face turns ghostly white.

"Anything you can tell me about her could help in the investigation."

Alan remains quiet and visibly upset for a few more seconds.

"Are you OK? Can I get you something?"

Alan recovers slowly. "I'm very sorry. She was a good employee."

"Like I said, anything you can tell me about her could be helpful to the investigation."

Alan is unable to advance his thoughts any further for a brief time. Then he repeats, "I'm very sorry."

"Take your time. Anything, even if it seems to be insignificant could help."

"How did she die?"

"The cause of death is still under investigation. We're not sure. You do remember something, don't you."

Alan's mind begins to return to normalcy. He wonders about telling what he knows about Charles and Denise, so he hesitates for a few more seconds.

"Mr. Jessup, I know you know something. Don't obstruct this investigation, don't protect someone. Help me do my job."

"Something very strange happened here a short time ago, right before Denise resigned. It might not be relevant to your investigation."

"Let me decide. What happened?"

Alan looks away for a short time, and then refocuses on her. "I told him I'd keep it between him and me. I gave him my word."

"If you conceal information that is important to this investigation, you can be held legally responsible. You can go to jail."

Alan answers, "Yes, I'm aware of that, but I gave him my word, I promised him."

Cardinale leans toward him. "Don't make this harder on yourself than it already is. There is something you know that could help me, don't you."

Alan takes in a deep breath of air and lets it out with a single puff. "OK, here's what I'll do." He clears his throat. "I'll ask him to talk with you. He'll decide what to say, if anything."

"That's not going to get you off the hook as a possible accomplice if he does not cooperate, but if that's what you want to do, then I'll go along with it for now. Who is he?"

"He's someone who I just recently hired. I'll call him to join us." He waits for a signal from her.

Cardinale nods her head affirmatively. "Do it."

Alan reaches for his phone, dials a two digit extension, and a few seconds later says, "Charles, I need to talk with you about something. Come to my office." He pauses. "No, it can't wait for later. It's very important." Another pause. "Yes, thanks." He disconnects the phone.

"What's his name?" she asks.

"Charles Westfield."

The next minute passes slowly, and then Charles steps into Alan's office.

"Oh, excuse me. I thought you were alone. Should I come back later?" Charles looks first at Alan and then at Cardinale.

"No, come in. And close the door." Alan hears his voice quiver.

Charles feels his stomach churn a little. He suddenly flashes back to the time he was let go from his previous job. He wonders if it is going to happen again. "Yes." After shutting the door, he takes a seat. His smile is weak and he knows it. "Are you firing me?"

"No. It's something else."

"Oh, I see."

"I don't think you do." Alan glances at Cardinale. "This is Detective Cardinale." He shifts back to look at Charles. "She is investigating a case that needs our help. I thought you might help her." Alan hears his own voice tremble a bit.

Charles thinks his heart just stopped pumping. For a short second, he is not sure where he is. A deep swallow brings him back to his senses. Then something suddenly dawns on him. "Has something happened to my wife and daughter?"

Alan answers first, "No, it's not your family."

Charles lets out a sigh of relieve. "Then who is it?" Charles is confused.

Cardinale jumps into the conversation. Her voice is calm. "I understand your last name is Westfield. Is that right?"

He nods, "Yes, that's correct." He looks at Alan with eyes opened wider than normal.

"I understand you know Miss Denise Cameon. Is that correct?" She takes out a notebook. "I'll want to jot down a few notes, if you don't mind."

Charles answers, "No, no, that's OK with me." All the while he tries to figure out what the meeting is really about. He looks at Alan for a clue but all he sees is a blank stare.

"How well did you know her?"

Charles feels as if his heart stopped beating and his breathing has just come to an end. He does not hear any noise around him. Then he comes back to his senses. "I'm sorry, can you repeat the question?" His mouth suddenly feels dry.

She breathes out and then pinches her lips. "How well did you know Miss Denise Cameon?"

Charles clears his throat, and glances at Alan. "What is this about?"

"Go on, it's OK to tell the truth." Alan nods his head. He feels more poised now that the pressure is off him.

Charles frowns, "Well, she was the Director of Human Resources. So, in that capacity she interviewed me for the job, and …" He pauses to clear his throat and then continue. "… conducted a new hire orientation for me. When I reported to work on my first day, I was told she had left the company."

Cardinale glances at Alan, and then returns to look at Charles. "That's it?"

Charles hears his own deep breathing. He looks at Alan for support, or at least a signal as what to say next. "What's going on here?"

"You should tell Detective Cardinale everything, just as you told me," Alan says with conviction.

Charles raises his voice. His eyes glare towards Alan. He sounds like a young kid. "You promised not to tell anyone, you promised!"

"I have not told anyone anything. That's why I asked you to meet with the Detective. It is very important. She is investigating Denise and I think you should cooperate."

Charles turns towards Cardinale, "What did she do?"

Detective Cardinale, "It's not what she's done. It's what's happened to her."

Charles glances at Alan confused.

Cardinale clarifies. "She was found dead in the desert a few days ago. I am investigating it."

Charles remains quiet for a short time, in shock from the news. Then he exclaims, "Oh no!"

Cardinale continues, "So you see, any information that you have might help me figure out what happened?"

Charles asks, "How did she die?"

Cardinale says, "We don't know." She pauses, "What do you know that I should know? Anything, even if it seems not worth mentioning, could help."

Alan adds, "I haven't said anything about what you

told me. I've kept my promise. But I think you should tell the Detective all about it, just like you told me. It might be of no relevance, but on the other hand, it might be very important."

"But you advised me earlier to keep this a secret, just between the two of us."

"The situation has obviously changed. Denise is dead."

Charles' head begins to swirly. Thoughts bump into each other in erratic motion, not making sense one way or another. He feels slightly dizzy so he takes in a deep breath of air to calm down. Finally, with his head tiled downward, he manages to say, "I don't have anything to offer. I'm sorry, I just don't."

Detective Cardinale glares at Alan. "Maybe we should all go downtown to talk about this."

Alan says, "Charles, you've got to tell her, or else …"

Charles interrupts, "Or else what?"

"Or else I will feel compelled to tell her everything that you told me, including the video." Alan is upset.

With renewed confidence Charles says, "You don't have any proof of anything, either a conversation or a video."

"That doesn't matter to me. Didn't you hear Detective Cardinale. Denise is dead! I'll still tell the Detective what you've told me," Alan is adamant.

Charles crosses his arms and remains silent.

Alan continues. "Damn it Charles, Denise is dead and you have information about you and her that might help the Detective solve the case! Tell her what happened between you and Denise! Go on, tell her!"

Cardinale switches glances back and forth between

Alan and Charles as if she is watching a tennis match. Annoyed at where the conversation is headed she interrupts. "I'll charge both of you with obstructing this investigation. I'll book you and let you sit in jail for a while until you both decide to cooperate." She looks back and forth between the two men. "Is that what you want?"

"If this comes out, my marriage will end." Tears begin to appear at the corners of Charles' eyes. "My daughter will hate me forever. I'll be alone, all alone."

It doesn't take Cardinale very long to piece a few bits of information together. "So, you and Denise had an affair, is that it?" Cardinale nods her head. "Then she dumped you. You felt so angry that you killed her." She nods her head again, and then leans towards Charles. "Or maybe she threatened to tell your wife. Either way, you killed her. Is that what happened?"

Charles straightens his body, and words flow out uncontrollably. "No, it was nothing like that! She came on to me, unexpectedly, and she videoed the whole thing! I told Alan everything. I even showed him the video. He's the one who told me to keep it quiet. He's the one who erased the video from the laptop. I'm the victim here, not her."

Cardinale turns to Alan, "Is that what happened?"

"Yes, that's right."

She asks, "Nothing to add?"

Alan looks at her, "I made a copy of the video for him to keep." Then he returns to look at Charles. "I don't know if he still has it."

Cardinale asks Charles, "Do you still have a copy of the video?"

Charles hesitates, prepared to lie, but changes his mind. "Yes, one copy. It's hidden away."

"I'd like to see it." Cardinale waits for a response that is long in coming.

Charles nods his head in frustration, "Sure, what the hell. It's all out now."

"Not really," Cardinale clarifies.

Charles looks her way, "What do you mean?"

"The video and what you've just said won't go any further than those who are investigating Miss Cameon's death."

Charles eyes brighten a little. "So, you won't tell my wife or daughter?"

"Not if we can help it, but you might have another opinion."

Charles nods his head.

Cardinale says, "Yes, it might be better coming from you, not from someone else." She pauses and then continues. "It's probably best if you come with me to the station when I look at the video. There's a good chance I'll have a few more questions to ask you."

Lines on Charles' forehead deepen. "Like what?"

"I don't know but there might be something I see or hear while I watch the video that will trigger a question. It's probably better we talk in private. No sense in getting Mr. Jessup any more involved than he has to." She glances at Alan and then returns to look at Charles.

Charles repeats the question, "Like what?"

Cardinale remains silent for a short time but then Charles interrupts before she can clarify. "You don't think I had anything to do with Denise's death?"

"It's my job just to get all the facts."

"I absolutely had nothing to do with her death, absolutely nothing!"

"Mr. Westfield, calm down. Let's talk about this at the station." Cardinale's voice is not persuasive enough.

A question pops into Charles' mind. "How did she die?" Charles looks back and forth between Alan and Cardinale. All he sees are two stone-faced people. His eyes widen. "Was she killed? Is that how she died?" Charles looks back and forth between Alan and the Detective. "Is that it?"

Cardinale asks, "Why would you say that?"

"Because you're treating me like a murder suspect."

Cardinale cocks her head to the side, "What do you want to tell me?"

"I'm telling you I had nothing to do with Denise's death!" Charles glares at her.

Alan decides to get into the conversation. "Charles, look at me."

Charles slowly turns his face towards Alan.

"The Detective already said the investigation is not complete and all she is doing is getting the facts." Alan shifts his glance towards Cardinale. "Isn't that what you said?"

Charles interrupts. "But she thinks I had something to do with Denise's death." He looks at Cardinale, "Isn't that right?"

"Like I said before, I'm just gathering the facts. We really should talk at the station." Cardinale stands. "Come on, let's get the video and go."

Almost out of control, Charles shouts, "I'm not going anyplace with you unless I have a lawyer!"

"If that's what you want, then you have the right to

one. But you are not being accused of anything. All I want to do is to see the video and talk a little more. That's all."

"I don't believe you." Charles crosses his arms. "I don't have the video. I destroyed it." He looks away to no particular spot in the room. His mind wildly races to unaccustomed places in the hope of finding a place of sanctuary. He wants the entire situation to end and never return, but realizes that is not possible now. The bird is out of its cage.

"I think you need to start believing me. Right now, I'm the only one who can help you get out of the mess you're in. You can take your chances with someone else or try to go it alone, but I know one thing for sure." She pauses. Once she sees Charles' eyes widen with interest she continues. "If you've done nothing wrong then you have nothing to worry about."

"OK." He presses his lips tightly together. "But I don't have the video."

Ω Ω Ω Ω Ω

The police station has a no smoking policy. The air is free of cigarette smoke smell, and there are no ashtrays. Most people like it that way, a few others prefer it to be the way it was. Too bad for those who want it returned to the old times.

Detective Cardinale sits in a metal chair across the table from Charles Westfield. She studies him.

Charles glances away and takes in a deep breath. "I haven't done anything wrong." He resets his glance towards her.

"Look, I'm not trying to get you to say something that isn't true. You've got to believe me." She thinks there is more to his story than what he has already shared. "I'm here to help you, not to hurt you."

"Yeah, you've said that before."

"Listen, I'm not trying to sweet-talk you, but you've got to trust me. I'm your only hope for setting the record straight."

He takes in a deep breath. "Listen, I've got a wife and daughter whom I really love. I don't want them to know any of this. They'd, well … I don't know what they'd do if they found out about Denise and me."

"But you've already said that she was the aggressor, and you were the victim. Right?"

"Yeah, right, but how many people will believe that. Come on."

"Too bad you destroyed the video. It would have cleared up all of this."

Charles looks away again. He changes his position in the chair. His thoughts are interrupted when someone enters the room.

"Detective, can I see you for a moment?" A plainclothes detective glances between Charles and her.

"Sure." Cardinale looks at Charles. "Give me a second. I'll be right back."

"I'm not going anyplace." Charles tries to judge the interruption, wonders if there is any truth to it, or if it is just another police ploy to get him rattled.

Cardinale steps outside the room.

Ω Ω Ω Ω Ω

"We found the weapon that killed the woman."

Cardinale says, "I'm listening."

"It was a throwaway .22 caliber semiautomatic pocket revolver."

Cardinale interrupts. "It holds six cartridges in its chamber. It's a small gun but still packs the power to end someone else's life with just one shot to the right place."

"It only took one shot. After the single bullet entered her temple, the gun still had five rounds left to be used. That wasn't necessary since she was dead instantly."

"Anyway to trace the gun?"

"No, the gun's serial number was filed away to prevent tracing the weapon back to its owner. The revolver was in the right hand of the deceased to imply she had taken her own life. However, there was no gunshot powder residue, blood or trace evidence on her hands or under her finger nails."

Cardinale says, "She probably never fired a gun before."

"Probably never went to be trained to use a revolver."

Cardinale summarizes. "So, this woman did not die from a self-inflicted gunshot, nor was it accidental. Someone with intent did her in. She did not die randomly. Her death was not a mistake. Is that the bottom line?"

"Yes, pure and simple."

Ω Ω Ω Ω Ω

Cardinale returns to the interrogation room to finish talking with Charles. She holds two bottles of water. "Here I brought you some water. I thought you might want it. I sure can use it to quench my thirst." She hands him a closed plastic container of water.

His expression changes. He is surprised, and then he nods. "Thanks."

"It's a peace offering, my gift to you." She smiles and takes a sip from the other bottle in her hand.

Charles untwists the cap and then takes a long gulp from the bottle given to him.

Then there is silence for a short time.

"The detective who I just talked with gave me an update on Miss Cameon's death."

Charles' stomach suddenly feels hot.

"He said she was murdered, but it was meant to look like a suicide."

Charles stares at her, words nowhere to be found.

"I think it's about time you tell me everything. It will be much easier on you if you're honest about what happened."

"What?" It is all he can find to say.

"Denise Cameon was murdered and her body was dumped in the desert to look like a suicide. Tell me about it. Why did you kill her? Was it to keep her silent about the affair? Did she threaten to tell your wife and daughter? Was that why you killed her?" In assessing Charles, she finds him not blinking, frozen-like in a motionless stage.

Then Charles raises his eyebrows, his mind no longer iced-up. "I-I'll show you the video. I-it'll prove she was the aggressor. I-I didn't do anything to her." The bottle of water falls from his hands and hits the floor. Clear liquid spills on the floor.

She has little reason to believe that the man in front

of her killed Denise Cameon, but a good prosecutor along with a poor defense attorney could persuade a jury to believe something quite different. She realizes she does not have all the facts and is gambling with her decision not to hold him but she is willing to take that risk. "Where is the video?"

"I-it's at home. I've hidden it."

"Then you've got to get it right now so I can see it."

Charles nods his head several times in agreement. "Of course, I'll get it right now." He stands ready to leave.

"Not so fast."

He frowns.

"I'll drive you home, and wait in my car. Then we'll both return to the station to watch it together."

"That'll work. Cass is working and Scarlet Rose has after school activities. Yes, that'll work."

She knows she has no evidence to hold him in custody, so she bluffs, "You owe me. I hope you appreciate what I'm doing."

Charles nods, "I know. I won't forget."

"I'll hold you to it. Now, let's get going."

CHAPTER 6

Once the meeting ends, Cass steps outside the conference room to walk towards her office. She glances at her watch surprised the meeting lasted as long as it did. She raises her eyebrows to hurry along. "Never enough time in the day," she whispers just loud enough for a nearby employee to hear.

"You can say that again."

She turns to see a coworker close by. "Where does the time go?" She shakes her head sideways.

"No place that I know." He grins. "See you later." He walks in another direction.

After she enters her small office, she notices a blinking yellow light atop the company's phone. "Great, more messages to get to." Standing alongside her desk, she leans over to retrieve the incoming messages. In listening to each one she assesses their level of importance. Suddenly her eyes open wider than normal to one particular message. Her mind temporarily goes blank and then quickly recovers. Slowly she sits in her chair to think about what to do. She uses her cell phone to call Charles.

"Charles?" Her voice is strained with emotion.

He recognizes the caller from Caller ID. "Yes, what's up?" He is not concentrating on much other than his troubles with the police right now. He sits in the backseat of the police car, cell phone pressed tightly against his ear.

Her throat constricts.

There is an awkward pause before Charles repeats the question. "What's up?"

Cass presses her free hand against her chest. The question sticks into her heart as if she had just been stabbed with a knife. She looks outside the office window and suddenly feels unprepared to go on. She feels unsteady as her body tilts to the side. Images of her daughter flash through her mind. She regains her mental state of balance. "I've got to work late tonight. I wonder if you would fix dinner for you and Scarlet Rose. I'll grab something myself here at work."

"Sure, I suppose that'll work. Sorry you've got to work late." He feels relieved of the seemingly unimportant request.

"I love you," Cass says, almost too softly to be heard by Charles and her.

"I love you too. Hurry home after work."

As soon as she disconnects the phones, she realizes it was a mistake. She had not imagined the intensity of the after-feeling to pretend to the job commitment and to withhold the real reason.

Charles slowly returns his cell phone to his pocket. He notices Cardinale eyeing him through the rear view mirror. "My wife. She's going to be working late."

Ω Ω Ω Ω Ω

She tries to knock on the door but her hand does not cooperate. Then she shakes her head sideways unsure what she should do. She steps away from the door and then stops. After taking in a deep breath of air, she steps towards the hotel guest room door again. Cass knocks twice, not as firm as she is capable.

"Coming."

She recognizes Mike's voice and is immediately prepared to pull back.

The door opens. She remains in the hallway.

"I wasn't sure I was going to come." Cass' voice is unsteady.

"I knew you would." Mike smiles and reaches out for her. "You look great. I was in town and couldn't pass up the opportunity to be with you."

"I'm not here for the reason you think."

"Oh, why are you here?"

Her voice is steady and unwavering. "I don't want to see you again. Stay away from my daughter and husband. I want you out of my life."

"Come in. We need to talk about that."

"No, I'm staying outside. Keep away from me and my family."

Mike steps back a few paces. "I think you want to come in. Don't act against your feelings."

She steps inside the guest room.

"Close the door."

She pushes the door shut. All she hears is sound of the door close.

Mike says, "That's more like it." He moves deeper into the room.

Cass follows him without saying a word.

"It's weird how some things happen. Know what I mean?"

Cass answers, "No I don't."

"If you want to win, you've got to stay in the game. I'm not saying you always win, but you've got to at least stay in the game for any chance of winning."

She steps back and looks at him directly in the eyes, "What's that suppose to mean?"

"Persistence, that's what it means. You've got to be persistent if you want anything in life."

"I think you work too hard at that. Don't work so hard."

"Sorry, it doesn't happen that way. You've got to work hard at whatever you want to get, whatever gives you satisfaction."

"What do you really enjoy? What's your satisfaction?"

"What do I enjoy? Isn't that obvious?"

"No, that's why I asked. What do you want and what satisfies you? It isn't obvious to me."

"Being with you, that's what I want and enjoy the most." He gives her another big smile. "I thought it was clear.

"Really, is that all you want?" She feels her body tense. She glares at Mike.

"You look mad. Are you?"

"I'm pissed at you?"

"You shouldn't be pissed at me. I'm the one who loves you. What do you really enjoy?"

Cass is caught off guard with the question so she thinks awhile. "Funny, I can't think of anything much. I mean … I go to work, come home to my family, go to sleep, and repeat the same process." She pauses and then continues. "But I'm not saying I don't love my family. I really do, especially my daughter. But that's different."

"Yes, I think so. It is different. I've met your family. Your daughter is great. I know I've never met Scarlet Rose before, but there is something about her that makes me think I know her. Ever have that happen to you?"

Cass' lips start to quiver. "I-I guess, but nothing comes to mind right now." She wonders to herself why she is with Mike rather than her family. "Maybe you need a different kind of joy in your life."

"I don't think so."

Cass turns halfway around. "I'm going. Don't contact me and my family ever again."

"You want to make love?"

She stops halfway around. Her face turns a light color of red.

He says, "You're blushing?"

"Don't be so obvious," she says.

"Why? You've got to show people what you want. You've got to make it obvious. You've got to act on what you want because no one is going to do it for you."

Cass asks, "You want sex. I know that, but what do you really want?"

"Haven't I been obvious?"

She smirks his way.

He ignores her looks. "First of all I want you all to myself."

She blushes again.

"Do you want to know my philosophy of life?"

She shrugs her shoulders, "Not necessarily."

"I'll tell you anyway. You've got to take control of life,

take what belongs to you and even what isn't yours but what you want."

"The first part I agree, but the second part, I don't agree."

"Cass, I think you do. I think that's why you keep coming back to me when I call."

"Huh?"

"I'm not afraid to grab for what I believe is mine even if it means breaking a few conventional rules. And, I think you are the same."

"That's idiotic, I don't think so," Cass shakes her head sideways.

"You really haven't changed much as a kid. You know, the time you impersonated a boy to get on the baseball team. That took real guts. I'm real proud of you for doing that."

"How do you know that?"

"It's my business to know things, and I know what you want."

Cass frowns, "What is it you think I want?"

"I'll tell you. You want someone to enjoy you, to take you to another level of love, to go places you never even dreamed of going." Mike pauses, steps forward and holds her face in his hands. "Would you like me to do that?"

Without hesitation, Cass disagrees, "No." She steps away.

"I think you do, or else why would you be here with me? You know what happens when we are together. We long to be with each other, to feel each other, to smell the aroma of each other. You enjoy how I make love to you. There is no one else who can please you the way I do. You know all this, yet you deny it. Stop rejecting the truth.

Act on your feelings. You can't deny them and you always show them. We need each other and we belong together, forever."

Ω Ω Ω Ω Ω

"This better be good." Scarlet Rose teases her father. "And you're going to test it first before I try it."

Charles smiles at his daughter, "It's my gift to you." He takes a bite of leftover meatloaf. "Fantastic. I might not share, it's so good."

"Right," she jokes back. "I'm just going to wait a few seconds to see if you keel over or something."

Charles fakes a dizzy spell. "Oh, no. I'm not feeling well."

"Don't quit your day job. You'd make a terrible actor." She reaches to move a large salad bowl to the dinner table. "While you're at it grab the olive oil and balsamic vinegar for the dressing."

"You sound just like your mother." Charles pauses, "And I love it. I love you both."

She asks. "Anything new happen at work?"

Charles feels his throat constrict but quickly recovers. "No, just getting accustomed to how they do things around the place." He swallows. "Anything new at school?"

Ω Ω Ω Ω Ω

"Christ, that was fantastic." Mike slowly shakes his head as he looks towards the ceiling.

Cass lays flat in the bed alongside Mike. She remains quiet.

He smiles and then continues. "And you've done a great job raising Scarlet Rose."

She wrinkles her forehead. "Let's not talk about her."

He ignores Cass. "Yes, she is going to be as wonderful as her mother."

She looks his way and raises her voice. "Mike, I asked you to stop talking about her!"

Mike closes his eyes and continues to disregard her. "Her fate was already set. Charles had nothing to do with it. He's only riding along, at least up until now."

She does not want to stay on the topic. Cass sits up in bed and glares at Mike. "Did you hear me? I said stop it!"

Mike looks her way. He grins. "I figure it's time for me to rejoin the family."

Cass moves away from him a bit. She feels frightened but is not totally sure why until Mike clears it up.

Mike believes this is the perfect time, so he decides to get down to business. "I know about her."

Cass opens her mouth to speak but nothing comes out at first. Then she says, "Huh?"

He sits up in bed. "Scarlet Rose is our daughter. I'm the father."

"You don't know what you're talking about!"

"We both know the truth. She's our child. I suspected it when I first met her, and then only after a few times alone with her, I was positively sure. She's beautiful, just like her mother. And her name, it's so appropriate." He smiles.

"You're wrong and I don't want to talk about it! She's my child, and I won't let you do anything to jeopardize that, so help me God!" She does not blink for quite a while. Her glare is ice cold.

"Cass, deny it to me all you want, but you know the truth and so do I."

She does not need to continue the conversation to know anymore, yet she carries on. "What's your reason for telling me this lie? What do you want from me?"

"It's not complicated, actually very simple."

"What is it?"

"I want you, me, and Scarlet Rose to be a family."

Her body immobilizes.

"That's right, to be one big happy family."

"You are totally out of your mind." Cass regains a little body mobility as she steps onto the floor. "This is a joke, right?"

"You don't wish it was, I know. It's the truth and we both know what needs to be done."

Cass is more than angry, she is furious. "You actually think my daughter is yours? That's a laugh! You walked out on me, or have you forgotten! I was left all alone to raise her without a father! You have no idea how I had to live, to lie, to … to…!" She is not able to finish the sentence.

He remains upright in bed. "I know you're upset, but in the long run it's best for all of us. Charles will understand when we tell him."

"Your wires are crossed!" She shakes her head sideways. Anger still blazes deep inside her. "Nothing like that is going to happen!"

"I've got to hand it to you."

She frowns.

He clarifies, "Your secret lifestyle all these years,

keeping to yourself who the real father is. But it wasn't too difficult to dig up the facts. I found out all sorts of things about your life, your parents, and more."

The bareness of her life to him suddenly makes her feel despondent. She shakes her head sideways, dejected, hopeless, and sad. She feels as if a thick gray haze has come from out of the blue to surround her. Cass begins to weep.

Mike slowly gets out of bed and heads towards Cass. "Don't cry. This is a time to celebrate. We'll be together just as it was meant to be, should be."

"Get away from me! You're crazy!"

"Did you really think you could keep it secret forever?" He waits for a response that does not come so he continues. "And why do you continue to sleep with me?" He pauses again and with the same result. "I'll tell you. Down deep inside you want me back in your life. You've always loved me. You know it and I know it. You can no longer live two lives, and I'm not going away."

Cass stares, motionless and wordless.

He stops only a few feet from her, gazes at her naked body. Then he smiles. "I've got a big house. Yeah, it'll be just fine, the three of us."

"You're not even hearing me! Are you deaf? And what the hell is that smirk all about?"

He heads for a chair where his clothes lay. "I think it'd be better if you told him to leave, not me. But, if you want, I'll have a talk with him. It's up to you." He starts dressing. "He's called me a few times to talk about Scarlet Rose. It might be time to call him back."

"Don't you dare!"

"It's only good manners to return phone calls." He smirks.

"I'm not telling him anything of the kind and neither are you!"

"Then you leave me no choice." He sits in the chair to put on his shoes.

"Don't you dare or else, so help me, …!"

He looks up, waits for her to finish the sentence. When she does not he says, "What will you do?"

"I'll kill you, I promise, I'll kill you and enjoy it!"

"It's been tried before." He stands. "I think you should get dressed. It's getting late and I've got to go." He grabs his coat and heads for the door. Then he turns to look around. "I don't have a lot of patience. You've got until the end of the month to do it." He opens the door and leaves her alone in the room.

"Fuck you!" It is all she can think of saying.

Mike does not stick around to hear her. What he hears instead is the click of the door closing behind him. He casually walks towards the elevator.

In the silence, alone, Cass feels isolated. Different shades of darkness cloud her thinking. She slowly sits in a nearby chair, but only for a short time. Motionless only calls greater attention to her condition. She stands again, and then walks around until she finds herself in the bathroom. She decides to take a long hot shower.

After less than a minute of hot water pouring over her body she holds her breath. She keeps precious air inside her lungs as long as possible before she releases. Cass begins to think more clearly. She realizes how much she underestimated the power of Mike's sexual magnetism at a time when she was most vulnerable. She did not imagine that a few flings could become habitual. And now that she knows his true intentions, she is at a lost about what next to do. But one thing is sure for now. She does not intend to tell Charles or Scarlet Rose about any of this regardless of how desperate she feels.

Ω Ω Ω Ω Ω

She is chilled by the short walk to her car. There is a slight rain. Once inside the vehicle, she starts the engine and waits a short time to let it warm up. Then she flips on the car's heater, and slowly drives off. The night's darkness and damp weather provide sufficient backdrop to make her feel miserable. She hears the windshield wipers sway back and forth to clear up the wet spots.

"Now what?" she says aloud. With no immediate answer Cass shrugs her shoulders and continues to drive in a robotic mental condition. Time passes without much recollection.

Eventually, she sees small lights up ahead that illuminate the edges of a driveway. She pulls into the paved pathway to park the car, and then she shuts off the engine. The headlights remain in effect for a short time until its timer gives the go-ahead to automatically turn off. She remains seated for a while. Rain drops continue to fall on the windshield to remind her of the gloom she feels.

She steps outside into the night. The driveway is wet and a little slippery so she cautiously walks towards a door alongside the garage. She feels chilled again and even more exposed of her hidden secret. Moisture clings to a few branches of nearby trees to remind her there is hope to make it all right. But she wonders if she has the strength to do it.

Quietly she opens the door and steps inside the garage. She hesitates before moving on. Cass reaffirms her commitment to keep her secret hidden from Charles and Scarlet Rose. She has no intention of revealing anything about her and Mike. She puts on a happy smile, the best she can summon for now. She proceeds to a single step that leads to a kitchen door.

Inside the kitchen, she smells warmed up meatloaf. The combination of ground beef, sausage, and oregano fill the air. She smiles. A muffled sound makes its way to her ears. She hears a movie in the background playing softly. After tossing her wet coat on a chair, she flips off her shoes and quietly walks into the living room.

At that very moment she realizes how very fortunate she is to have a loving husband and daughter. Scarlet Rose and Charles sit close to each other on the couch. Scarlet Rose rests her head on her father's shoulder. Cass snuggles between them to feel the comfort of their closeness. She kisses Charles on the cheek and then does the same with Scarlet Rose.

Scarlet Rose says, "Hi mom."

Charles says, "Hello honey."

She tells herself that everything is under control, and the best thing she can do is to act normal.

CHAPTER 7

The next morning, Cass wakes slowly. Her eyes feel heavy and her eyelids do not want to cooperate. They remain closed for a short time. Her body feels as if she has been a punching bag for a ten round fight. "Uh," she manages to say. Automatically she extends her left arm to touch Charles, but to her surprise her hand rests on the sheet. She manages to move her head to the right to check out the time, but that move is not successful. Her sight is blurred. Cass rubs her eyes a few times, and then with some difficulty leaves the comfort of the warm bed to sit up. She stretches her arms over her head and then gives it another shot at checking out the time. The numbers on the digital clock indicate 10:41 am.

"Holy-moly," she whispers.

The realization unnerves her. She estimates she has slept at least twelve continuous hours. Cass tries to get her body into a higher gear but that proves to be a big challenge, so she lets her body flop back into bed for a little longer.

"Cass, are you awake yet?"

She hears Charles call out to her. "Uh, yeah, I'm

getting up now." This time she manages to get out of bed for good. She slowly walks to the bathroom to ready herself for the day. She is shocked at the reflection in the mirror. Her face is puffy, both eyes are reduced to thin slits, and her skin is almost the color of bleach.

Troubled, with an aching body, she reaches for her clothes, dresses, and makes her way downstairs. She feels hungry.

As she enters the kitchen she notices Charles reading the morning paper. A hot cup of coffee sits in front of him. She moves close to him, bends over and kisses him on the cheek. "I don't know what happened. I was exhausted."

Charles turns to look. He is slightly shocked at her weary appearance. "You've been working too hard. Maybe you should take a few days off. The rest will do you good." He stands to put his arms around her. "Here, take a seat. What do you want for breakfast? Just name it and I'll make it."

"Coffee for starters, and then a lot of anything. I'm starved."

"Coming right up." He moves to fill a mug of hot coffee.

"I don't even remember going to bed last night. The last thing I remember is sitting alongside you and Scarlet Rose during the movie."

"You fell asleep pretty quickly after you sat down. I carried you upstairs. You were out cold." He returns to her side. "Here's the coffee."

She nods her head sideways, baffled about it all. Then she slowly sips the coffee. "Ah, this is just what I need."

"Bowl of fruit, scrambled eggs, and toast?" He asks.

"Perfect. I love you."

"Coming right up." Charles turns to prepare her meal.

While the act of cooking is soothing, the smell is more comforting.

Cass turns to glance at the morning paper. As she brings the mug of coffee to her lips, she asks, "Where's Scarlet Rose?".

"Out with school friends. She said there's a school project due next Monday."

Cass takes a sip of coffee.

A few minutes of silence pass before Charles says, "I still haven't heard from Mike. I wonder what's up. Have you heard anything from him?"

Cass feels her heartbeat pickup. "No." The one word is all she is able to say.

"I really want to know why he was seeing our daughter behind our backs." Charles finishes off cutting an assortment of fresh fruit to put into a bowl.

She finds it difficult to continue the conversation, but knows she must. "Yeah, I guess we'll just have to wait to hear from him."

"Has Scarlet Rose heard from him?" He sets the bowl of fruit on the kitchen table in front of Cass.

She almost drops the mug of coffee but recovers in the nick of time. "She hasn't said anything to me." Cass wonders if he picks up the quiver in her voice.

He begins scrambling two eggs mixed with cheddar cheese and milk.

She feels her stomach churn and wonders how long she can keep her secret from him.

While he is doing his best to keep hidden from Cass the entire situation about Denise, he feels pulled in opposite directions about whether it is the best decision. His resolve to keep everything hidden lessens with each passing day. He continues to stare down at the frying pan as he stirs the ingredients with a metal whisk. Suddenly, and without conscious forethought, he blurts out, "Cass, I've got …"

At the exact same instant, Cass comes out with something similar, "Charles, there's something …"

Then there is silence, neither willing to finish off their thoughts.

"I'm sorry, you go first," Cass says, relieved to have been cut off.

"No, you go." Charles eyes widen. He too is thankful he was interrupted.

Another round of silence comforts them for a short time.

"It's nothing." He takes in a deep breath and then removes the pan from the gas flames. "This looks good." He walks towards an empty dish to slide the scrambled eggs onto.

"I'm still tired. I've already forgotten what I was going to say," she says.

He sets the dish containing the eggs on the table. "Yeah, we're two old folks losing our minds." He smiles and kisses her on the cheek.

"I'm happy to grow old with you. I love you so much." She feels a tear form in the corner of her eye.

He looks at her, and then at the plate of food. "Oops, I forgot the toast. Be right up." He quickly moves to the counter to slip two pieces of sourdough bread into a toaster.

Ω Ω Ω Ω Ω

"What if you're wrong and he really killed her?" Detective Briley looks at Detective Cardinale.

"I first thought he did it, my gut told me."

"What changed your mind?"

"Only circumstantial, no hard evidence whatsoever," she says. "We've got to look for real evidence."

"But there is motive," he adds.

"Sure. She could have threatened to tell his wife, and even his boss, in exchange for money or something else to remain quiet. But I've got to tell you, after I've spent some time with this guy, he doesn't seem to be the killer type."

Detective Briley continues. "Sure as hell, you and I know there are lots of guys who would consider silencing someone under these conditions."

"Maybe you should talk with him alone. You know, man to man. I've got no problem if you want to." She shrugs her shoulders. "I'm not perfect. Maybe there's something I missed."

"So, no problem, huh."

"None whatsoever. Here's the file. Check it out and give him a call. The case is cold as it now stands." She slides the file across the table.

Ω Ω Ω Ω Ω

Detective Briley enters Tommy's Restaurant. He looks around to spot Tommy, the owner, at the bar who motions him to come by for a shot of whiskey. As he walks past a few customers, he recognizes a few regulars from the evening crowd, nods his head and mumbles a few words that are not recognizable to anyone. No one listens to what's said, it's the intention that counts.

"Your booth is in the corner, just like you wanted." Tommy motions with his head to a particular spot a few yards away.

"Thanks." He grabs hold of the shot glass and then with one swallow throws the whiskey into his mouth. "Don't want any interruptions."

"No problem." Tommy pauses. "You want me to run a tab?"

"No."

"Tracy's working today." He grins at Briley.

Briley makes a face. "Great. Does she know I'm here?"

"Not from me."

Briley lets out a grunt. "Got a menu?"

"Why do you need a menu, this isn't the first time you've been here?"

"I'm meeting someone who hasn't been here before and he may want to check out the choices. Come on Tommy, give me a menu."

"Order the special, it's good. Roasted breast of chicken, mixed vegetables, and brown rice."

"I still want a menu."

"I'll have Tracy bring it to you." Tommy smiles.

Briley looks at the top of the bar. "She's got unrealistic expectations." Then he lifts his head to look at Tommy. "She's real nice, but I'm not looking for a long term relationship."

"Maybe you should tell her. The truth might hurt but it clears away the confusion."

"She knows I'm not married, never was, and that I don't think it is in the cards for me. I use my apartment for not much more than sleeping, showering, changing clothes and having a drink before I go to sleep. Sometimes I stay overnight at her place, not often. How much clearer do I have to be?"

"Evidently a lot more because either she doesn't get it or thinks she can convince you otherwise."

Briley shakes his head in frustration. "Fuck this! Just give me the fucking menu!"

Tommy keeps quiet.

Briley spots a menu at the corner of the bar, grabs it, and heads for the corner booth.

At a little past noon, Charles walks in. He looks around and heads to the bar where he was told he would meet Detective Briley.

Tommy knows the regulars. Charles is not one of them. So, he figures this is the guy Briley told him about. "In the corner booth." Tommy motions to where Briley waits.

"Yeah, thanks." Charles feels nervous but tells himself there is nothing to worry about. He did not kill Denise and he has no idea who did. He walks towards the booth. "Detective Briley?" He extends a hand to shake.

"Yeah, that's me. You must be Charles Westfield."

"Yes I am. I'm sorry I'm late. Traffic, you know."

"Sure, not a problem, have a seat." He waits for Charles to sit, and then continues. "Thanks for coming. I hope this place is OK with you instead of the station."

"Sure, I need to eat lunch anyway." Charles hears his voice quiver a little.

"Want a drink?"

"No thanks but go ahead if you want."

"Oh, no. I only drink at dinner after work, wine mostly." He pushes the menu towards Charles. "Here's the menu. Everything is good."

"You know what you want already?"

"Yeah, I've been here before. The daily special is great."

Charles takes a deep breath of air in and then lets it out. He begins to feel less nervous already. "What is it?" He places the menu flat on the table.

"Roasted chicken breast, mixed vegetables, and brown rice."

"Sounds great. I'll have what you're having."

Briley motions to Tommy with two fingers that gets the right response. Then he looks at Charles. "I just ordered us the special."

Charles remains quiet.

Tracy appears. "Hi Al." She looks at Briley with a bright smile. "How are you doing today?"

Briley limits the response to one word, "Fine."

"What can I get you to drink?" Tracy remains upbeat as she glances between the two men.

"I'll have coffee." He turns to Charles, "What do you want to drink, it comes with the meal."

Tracy interrupts, "As long as it's non-alcoholic."

Charles answers. "Coffee for me as well."

"Two coffees coming up." She smiles again at Briley, waits for a response that does not come, and then walks away.

"I hope you don't mind if we get into this right away. I know you've got to get back to work." He waits for Charles to answer.

"Whatever I can do to help." Charles fidgets in the booth.

"Detective Cardinale has already briefed me and I've reviewed the case, so I'm pretty much up to date. I've also seen the video with you and the deceased. I might add, as one man to another, she was quite a healthy looking woman." Briley grins just a little to see what response he gets from Charles. He notices Charles get embarrassed. "Sometimes my bluntness makes people a little uncomfortable. I'm sorry, but it's who I am."

Charles waves off the apology.

"I understand you were unemployed for a while before you were hired into your current company, is that right?"

"Yes, it's tough out there to find a new job, especially with so many people looking for so few positions. I think I was lucky."

Briley asks, "What's luck got to do with it? I assumed you were qualified for the position."

"I've discovered it's all about networking, it's who you know and who knows you."

"Are you saying you got the job because you knew someone?"

"Actually my wife."

"Oh, tell me about that."

Charles looks away for a second and then returns to face Briley. "It was real crazy. My wife went to her class reunion. One of her former schoolmates recommended me to an executive search firm who recommended me to my current employer. I would have never interviewed with this company if Mike hadn't passed my name along. Crazy, huh?"

"Mike is your wife's schoolmate?"

"Yeah, Mike Aviara. He's well connected, evidently knows lots of people. As far as I'm concerned he's the one responsible for me getting the job."

At the sound of Mike Aviara's name, Briley's eyes widen for a quick instance. He recognizes the name. He keeps his voice under control. "That's how it happens, just like you said, it's all about networking."

Tracy returns with two filled coffee cups. Without saying a word, she places each cup in front of Briley and Charles. She then quickly walks away.

Charles picks up the conversation. "We've had Mike over for dinner. He's met my daughter. We all like him very much."

"I see. It appears as if everything has turned out great for you."

"Yeah, it appears that way." Charles is less convincing than he would otherwise like to be.

"Ok, now Denise Cameon. Tell me about her."

"Not anything more I can add to what I've already told Detective Cardinale."

"So she just came onto you without any encouragement from you."

Charles lowers his voice. "I know you find that hard to believe. I mean ... she is, was, a good-looking woman, and I'm an average looking guy. Why would she come onto me?" Charles shrugs his shoulders. "Why would she video us? I really don't get it."

"People like her do those kinds of things because they're voyeurs. They get a high over sexual dominance and seeing themselves on video." Briley pauses and then continues. "And then there is the other reason." He waits to see the reaction from Charles.

Charles eyes widen. "And what is the other reason?" He feels his throat constrict.

"Blackmail." He pauses to let the word sink in. He sees Charles' eyes widen. Then he continues. "You seem surprised."

Charles clears his throat. "Well, sure."

"Tell me about it."

"What's there to say, I'm not a wealthy man. I'm not someone who can pull strings for other people. I'm well, just an ordinary guy."

"Maybe that wasn't the case, at least not according to her thinking." He waits for Charles to respond but silence is what remains. Briley continues, "In other words, she told you she wouldn't show your family the video in exchange for money, blackmail. This happens all the time. She figured you'd get the money someplace. That wasn't her problem. She figured you're the desperate one, not her."

Charles raises his voice. "But that didn't happen." Then his tone lowers. "She never said anything like that. In fact, she didn't say anything."

Briley clarifies. "It's really your word against her word." He pauses and then presses on. "In these types of situations, the payoff never ends. After the victim gives over the agreed upon money, they think everything is going to go away. But then there is a demand for another payoff, and then another and another."

"You think that's what happened, don't you."

"Did it?"

"No, it never happened."

"That's right, she was murdered."

"You don't still think I killed her, do you?"

"Look at it from my perspective. She threatened to show the video to your family if you didn't pay her off. You agreed to meet with her to exchange the video for the cash, but instead, you killed her. It's that simple."

Charles shakes his head. "Except that's not what happened. We never met after the, ah, thing, and she never asked for money. Nothing like that happened."

"But something did happen to her. She's dead. Somebody tried to make it appear to be a suicide, but she was definitely murdered."

Charles leans forward. "I didn't do it. You've got to believe me."

"Give me something to believe. It's just your word."

Charles looks away. "You only have my word, nothing else."

Briley leans forward, and nods his head up and down. "I'll be honest with you. I do believe you, I really do. But there's got to be more to it."

"What do you mean?"

"A woman without any criminal record was the HR Director for a respected company. For some reason she seduced you, and to boot, she videoed the entire thing. The video was still on her laptop because she never thought about deleting it. She was found in the desert with a bullet in her head but it was meant to look like a suicide. She never contacted you, never demanded anything from you, and I suspect, although you haven't mentioned this to me or anyone else, she never contacted your wife. Doesn't all of this seem a bit weird to you?"

Before Charles has a chance to answer, Tracy stands

alongside their table. This time she speaks. "Two specials." She sets two plates on the table. "Be careful, they're hot. Can I get you refills?"

Ω Ω Ω Ω Ω

Thirty minutes later, Charles and Detective Briley finish lunch.

Briley places his fork alongside a knife on the empty plate. "There are no other murder suspects."

"So, I'm no longer under suspicion?"

"That's right."

"I'm relieved to hear that." Charles says, "I wish I had more to tell you, but I don't."

"So do I, but be careful."

Charles frowns, "About what?"

"It's just my gut talking. After a while I listen more to it than my brain." Briley's face is serious looking.

"You're making me nervous."

"I want you to be careful. If that comes with nervousness, then that's how it is."

"Thanks for the advice." Charles glances at his watch, "I should be getting back to work. Are we done?"

"For now, sure, but I'm probably going to want to talk with you again. So, if you're planning to leave the area for any reason, let me know." He shoves a name card towards Charles. "Take this and call me if you think of anything else. I mean … anything regardless of whether you think it's important or not. OK?"

"OK." Charles pauses and then continues, "Are you going to talk with my wife or daughter about this?"

"Not if I can help, but it's quite probable at some

time later I might have to. So, you know what you have to do."

"What's that?"

"I think they'd rather hear it from you, not from me. Know what I mean?"

"Yeah." Charles understands but is not yet ready to divulge anything to his family. He dips into his wallet to pay his share of the bill. He empties his billfold by dropping a twenty dollar bill on the table. He reminds himself to stop off at the bank to get some cash. He stands without saying anything else and leaves Briley alone.

Ω Ω Ω Ω Ω

Outside the restaurant Charles is disoriented. He slowly walks to his parked car to reset his mental compass, and then remembers he used up all his cash. He looks around to spot an ATM to the right of a bank's entrance. He moves in that direction.

He takes out his ATM access card and slips it into the slot. A message appears on the screen to provide his PIN. He covers the keys with his left hand as he presses the appropriate keys with his right index finger. He waits for another message to offer him a menu selection. He decides to withdraw one hundred dollars.

He is shaken when a different message appears. ACCESS DENIED. SEE TELLER INSIDE.

He hears a whining sound. He waits for his access card to reappear, but it does not. He swallows hard.

Now inside the bank, he walks to the nearest teller. "Something is wrong. I can't get access to my checking account."

"You need to speak with one of our bank officers. I'll get someone to talk with you. Please stay here." She walks away for a short time.

Charles wonders if it is just an error or a piece of his world falling apart. Inner thoughts are interrupted.

"Hello, I'm Crystal Legite. Please come with me."

"Yes, of course." He follows her into a private office.

"Please, have a seat." She sits down. "You told our teller that you cannot access your checking account. Is that right?"

"Yes. I used my ATM card, typed my PIN and was about to withdraw some cash. But instead I got a message on the screen that denied access. My card is still inside the machine, it swallowed it."

"Do you have a photo ID so that I can check your account?"

"Yes, of course." He opens his wallet to remove a driver's license. "Here is my driver's license."

Crystal Legite searches the bank's data base. The process takes less than a minute. She nods. "Yes, I see what's happened."

"What is it, what's the matter?"

"Your account was temporarily frozen early this morning. It seems someone unauthorized tried to access your account." She looks up from her computer screen. "We sent you an e-mail notifying you of this."

"Do you know who did this?"

"No, I have no way of knowing that. The good news is no money was withdrawn but what is baffling is the unauthorized person tried to deposit money into your account."

"Deposit money?"

215

"Yes, deposit money. I've experienced all sorts of transactions, but I don't ever remember anyone who is not authorized trying to deposit money into someone else's account."

"What's next?"

"You should immediately change your PIN and your account number or numbers if you have multiple accounts with us. That's the safest thing to do."

"Can we do that now?"

"Sure, let's get started."

Ω Ω Ω Ω Ω

Later the same day Cass, Charles and Scarlet Rose eat dinner together at home.

Charles shakes his head sideways, confused. "That's the truth."

"But it doesn't make sense." Cass is as confused as he.

Scarlet Rose shrugs her shoulders. She takes a bite of salad and chews it nonchalantly.

"I know but it is the truth."

Scarlet Rose decides to get into the conversation. "Why would someone want to give you money?"

"Honey, that's what's so mysterious about this. We can't figure that out." Cass takes a sip of iced tea.

"The bank officer said she'd never seen this happen before, a first for her."

"I suppose I have to stop by the bank to fill out some forms for the new accounts and change my PIN." Cass looks at her plate to cut a piece of chicken. Then she glances at Charles. "Are you OK? You look sick?"

Wrinkles appear between his eyes. His worried expression suggests something is wrong. He turns to Cass. "There's something I've got to tell you."

"Of course. Do we need to be alone?"

"Oh, mom, come on. I'm old enough to hear whatever it is."

"Charles, do we?"

He smacks his lips and at first does not change his look. Then, slowly, he turns toward Scarlet Rose and back to Cass. Finally he finds the right words to use. "It's not pretty but she should stay."

"Yey," Scarlet Rose says in celebration. She centers her attention on her father, waits in anticipation of what he is about to tell.

"If you say so, go on. What is it you want to tell me?"

"I've told you about Denise Cameon, the HR Director."

"Yes, I remember. What about her?"

"I was the last one to see her, at least the last one from the office."

Cass' heart starts to beat up. She remains quiet.

"She helped me with the new hire paperwork, and got me into the system. You know how that is, you've done it a million times."

Scarlet Rose is let down. Her face sulks and she is moodily silent.

"After all the paperwork was completed, I left her to come home. There was no one else in the office, except her. I was the last one to see her that night." He stops short of the next thought. He begins to sense a churning in his stomach and a slow movement of acid up his esophagus. He quickly takes a gulp of water to settle down.

Cass looks on with increased tension. "You don't have to go on. Whatever it is you want to tell me can wait."

He waves her off. "No, this is important." He takes in a deep breath of air and then slowly exhales. He glances at Scarlet Rose who now shares her mother's concern. "I'll be alright." He smiles at his daughter.

"It's OK dad." She smiles back.

"Like I said I was the last one to see her that night. That was a mid-week night. You remember, don't you?" He glances at his wife.

"Yes. I also remember how jittery you were when you came home that night, but I figured it was all the excitement of finding a new job."

He pauses to take a deep gulp of air. "When I went to work on the following Monday, she wasn't there. At first I thought she was late, or had an appointment, or maybe was taking a personal day off. You know, it's not uncommon." He looks at them. Worry still creases his face. "Then Alan told me she had suddenly resigned due to a family matter. It had to be after meeting with me. Then he mentioned that he'd have to find her replacement. I thought of you."

"Me, why would you think of me?" Cass asks.

"Maybe you'd want to work there as the HR Director?" He shrugs his shoulders, "I don't know, I just thought of you."

"Probably not a good idea for both of us to work at the same company. Anyway, you've already told me this before. What else is there?"

"What's so important about this story?" Scarlet Rose

glances back and forth between her parents. "I don't get it, I'm bored."

Charles looks at his daughter and then readjusts to his wife. "A few days later, Alan told me Denise was found dead in the desert. The police think she was murdered."

Cass puts her hands to her mouth, "Oh no."

Scarlet Rose says, "Wow."

"An obvious person of interest was initially me." He lifts his shoulders. "In a way I understand why. I was alone with her the one night at work."

"But she resigned after that, so she had to have talked with Alan or someone else. You weren't the last person to see her."

"I know, but the police were considering everyone as possible suspects."

"Do they still suspect you?" Cass asks.

"No, I'm off the list. I don't have any …" Suddenly his throat constricts. He coughs. Then he manages to finish the sentence. "…reason."

There are a few moments of silence that seem to be endless.

Cass asks, "Are the police still investigating Denise's murder?"

"Yes, but there are no suspects."

Another lapse of conversation lasts a few seconds.

He decides to alter the subject so he says, "I still haven't heard from Mike since I left the messages."

Scarlet Rose interrupts, "Are we done with the murder?" She glances back and forth between her parents.

"Yes, I think so, at least for now. There isn't anything else to say." Cass nods her head towards her daughter.

Scarlet Rose looks disappointed. "Oh."

ΩΩΩΩΩ

The drive to the trailer park is depressing. Mike wonders why he is even taking the time to see her. She was not there for him when he was a boy, when he needed motherly love and support. He remembers her being in a stupor most of the time, too much vodka. He checks his car's clock and then refocuses on the drive.

When he got a phone call from one of her neighbors that she was fading fast, he almost hung up, thankful that she would be out of his life once and for all. That obviously did not happen. Does she still have power over him? He quickly concludes that is just how it is between mothers and sons.

Up ahead are several cars in a funeral procession. He slows down, not eager to pass the line of vehicles. It would only cause him to arrive at his destination that much faster. He flashes to a previous time when he sat in the backseat alongside his mother in a large black limousine on the way to his father's funeral. He did not have the tears to cry then, and he predicts the same situation will be repeated when his mother passes on. He knows he was not that great of a son to his parents, so maybe this is a sort of payback.

He slows down for a stop light up ahead. He taps his fingers on the steering wheel to an imaginary tune until he sees the signal light turn green. He returns to thinking about the upcoming meeting with his ill mother. He is unsure about what he will say to her since they have not been in contact for several years. He tells himself silently that saying hi and how are you doing sounds phony, yet that is the precise description of the relationship he and his mother have had all these years.

He drives a few more miles and then veers left for another mile past a small run down shopping center of small businesses. There are few cars in the parking lot, mostly of employees from the few stores still in business. He shakes his head sideways. It is not easy to successfully run a small business.

He drives another mile on a tree lined street. Immediately after the trees, Mike spots a small sign on the left side of the road, VIEW POINT. He slows down and takes a left turn. The road is unpaved.

He drives up a hill where the single lane dirt road turns into a Y. The car's tires seem to find each bump in the road. He spots the trailer homes on each side. A crooked sign indicates number addresses for each home. He sees what he is looking for and takes a right turn toward #155. He parks his car on the side of his mother's house, and then takes a long look at the place.

The trailer home is a light yellow-brown colored rectangular metal structure. He notices a few chips of paint flaking off the outside surface. The front wooden door is open but a patched-up screen door is closed that allows a slight breeze to enter the place. There is an overhang above the front door and a light bulb that is unlit. Mike notices one large window to the left of the door. Dark curtains are closed so he cannot see inside.

After a short internal struggle on whether to move out of the car or drive off, Mike makes his way to the front door. He steps on a chipped slab of concrete at the entrance. He stops just short of announcing his presence. His knuckles are frozen inches away from the door.

The internal battle reemerges. Finally he fights off the temptation to walk away and raps on the door. He waits for a signal.

At first there is no response, so he gives it another few taps. His voice is unenthusiastic. "Anyone home?" He stretches his neck to look through the screen door. He does not see anyone.

"The door's open. Come in whoever you are." Her voice is weak sounding.

Mike steps inside the trailer home, looks around at the messy conditions, and then eventually spots his mother. He takes in a deep breath at her scrawny appearance. He feels the beat of his heart pick up.

From inside the residence he notices the flat ceiling with a fan installed in the small living room. The honey colored linoleum floor is worn and the interior walls are painted china doll. To his right he sees a small kitchen area that is equipped with a small white stove, refrigerator, and sink. He suspects the bedroom and bathroom are in another part of the place.

"Just don't stand there, come closer. Let me see you." She manages to wave a fragile looking hand to summons him nearer.

Slowly he steps forward. "Yes."

From the cloth covered rocking chair, her face brightens at the sound of her son's voice in spite of it being only one word. With obvious discomfort she slowly extends both arms in the direction of Mike's tone.

He takes another step closer and then realizes she is having a difficult time seeing him. "I'm here."

She moves her arms towards his voice. "I can't see you, so come closer."

He takes hold of her hands, "I'm right here."

She squints. "You're all grown up. You're a man."

His voice is softer and sweeter than he thought it would be. "Yes I am." He sits alongside her.

"I didn't think you'd come," she admits.

"We haven't exactly been close."

"Yes, that's what I mean." She keeps a tight clench on his hands. "But you did come."

He decides being honest has no payoff, so he answers, "Of course."

"I wasn't the best mother to you, I know that, but I did the best I could." She puckers her lips. "I should have been better."

Mike feels a great amount of built up anger fighting to leap out at her. He tightens his grip around her hands for a split second, and then relaxes to resist losing control. "That was then." He decides to let it pass.

"Are you still angry with me?"

"Why would I be angry?"

"You can't fool your mother. I guess you are. I'm sorry."

"That was a long time ago."

"I could have been a better wife to your father as well. I miss him, even though I didn't cry when he died."

"Don't blame yourself. He was a difficult person to get along with. I should know."

She releases his hands, and slowly slumps back into the rocking chair. "I wanted to get in touch with you all these years. My only excuse was selfishness. I was waiting for you to do it first." She remains looking at him.

Mike nods in agreement. "I was so angry at the both of you. When he died I didn't even cry. I was actually pleased that he wouldn't be around anymore, controlling me."

"You had every right to be angry. I'm sorry." She looks his way in spite of not seeing him clearly. "After your father died, I nearly drank myself to death. I both loved him and hated him at the same time."

"So you understand how I felt," Mike says.

"Yes, but it's different now, isn't it."

"What do you mean?"

"I'm not smart enough to tell you or anyone else how to mourn or forgive, or for that matter, love. All I can say is do what's in your heart."

Mike feels closeness to his mother. He searches for something positive to say. "I've got good news to tell you."

"Yes, what is it?" She leans forward. Her voice sounds excited.

"I've met this wonderful woman who loves me as much as I love her. We're going to be married soon."

"That's wonderful. Have you set a date?"

"Not exactly, but it will be soon, very soon."

"But, it'll be too late for me to see any grandchildren. I'm losing life's battle faster as each day goes by."

"She has a wonderful daughter from a previous marriage."

Her voice turns to disappointment. "Oh."

"Her husband died several years ago. The girl and I get along very well. It's going to be a great family."

For a moment, she does not move or speak. Then she says, "There's a letter I've written to you but never mailed. Take it. It's on the table by the door." She closes her eyes and her body goes limp. Her thin hands rest on her lap.

Mike believes she has fallen asleep, so he stands, kisses her on the cheek, grabs the letter, and leaves.

Ω Ω Ω Ω Ω

Several days pass since his mother died. He hasn't had much sleep since then. If he could see his face it would look puffy and fatigued.

He pulls out of his pocket the letter his mother had written to him but never sent. His hands tremble just a little as he reads it again.

My darling son. I'm not doing well and I'm not sure how much longer God will keep me alive. It's HIS decision, not mine. I wish you were here so I could talk with you in person. I know I have not been a good mother to you, but I tried my best. Now I want to ask you one last favor. Is it OK with you? I hope it is OK. What I want is for you to show patience, be calm and understanding, and keep your temper under control. Don't get so hot over little things. I beg you to control your temper. It will get you into a lot of trouble, just like when you were a young boy. Remember? Will you do that for your mother? And one more thing. This is very important. I don't want a big funeral. I don't want people to come to my funeral who didn't come to see me when I was alive. I will always love you. God bless you. XXX Mother

He stares at the piece of paper for a few more seconds and then puts it back into the envelope. Then he shoves the envelope into his pocket. His expression is serious, and his gaze is narrow and focused.

He takes in a deep breath and refocuses on why he is

standing where he is. "I'll be damned to take a back seat to what's mine." Mike stands across the street from the Westfield residence. It is shortly after one in the morning, the same as two successive nights ago when he checked out the place. Nothing has changed except his determination. He is more resolved than ever before.

There is a light drizzle. He is slightly chilled by the early morning air and rain, so he blows air on his hands and then rubs them together to warm up. Then he reaches into a pocket of his wool coat to touch the .32 caliber gun. He grins at its cold metal feel.

He pictures snapshots of Cass in his head. It is almost like seeing her in the flesh but it is not the same as being with her. He is bound and determined to bring those images to life. What started as a distraction during the class reunion first turned into a motivation. By now, it is an obsession, an uncontrolled driving force that is more powerful than he ever imagined. Is it the truth that he loves her, or has he outgrown the truth and replaced it with something else? At this point in time the devil within him has taken over.

At this early hour of the morning he is alone. Not even a stray cat or dog is around. There is no sound of vehicles. It is as if life itself has deserted him. Nonetheless he still feels out in the open for everyone to see.

It is the nippiness in the air and not his nerves that makes him shiver a little. He tries not to look away from the structure but for some reason he glances toward an opened area to his right. His mind fast forwards to an impression of the three of them playing together, laughing and having a good time. He does not struggle to keep from smiling. He can't wait to be with Cass and Scarlet Rose as a family.

He takes a last look at his watch and decides it is time to put his plan into action. He has thought it over again and again. It now seems automatic to get on with it. Without looking to each side of the street, he steps off the curb and slowly walks closer to the house. He almost slips on the wet pavement, but quickly regains his balance.

As he approaches the building he feels confidence grow. This is not his first crime. He takes in a deep breath and another feel of the revolver inside his coat pocket.

He uses a small metal tool about the size of a fingernail file that fits most door locks. Mike twists the instrument four times inside the side door locking mechanism. He hears clicking sounds and then a final pop. It takes him less than two minutes to unlock the side door of the house. He shakes his head sideways wondering why most people do not invest in superior home security systems. Now inside, his memory of the downstairs interior comes back fast. He quickly estimates the layout of the upstairs before he takes the first step on the stairway.

A shadow from the living room crosses his path as he moves up the flight of stairs. He figures the worst part is over. The remainder is a slam dunk. He reaches for the .32 revolver. It does not take him long to reach the top of the stairs. He looks around to determine which way to proceed, and then he walks to his right.

At the entrance of the master bedroom he spots her sleeping. Mike gazes at Cass, smiles and feels pleased. Then it dawns on him she is alone. He pivots to his left and then to his right. Maybe Charles is someplace nearby. He frowns and listens for a sound to give away Charles' location. It is silent. Mike concludes it is just Cass and him in the bedroom, and that maybe she and Charles have separate bedrooms or perhaps Charles is away. It does not matter to Mike the reason. It is what it is.

He moves in her direction. Once nearby he tenderly touches her hair, lets it gently drift through his fingers.

She suddenly turns her body to the side and makes a slight grunting sound.

Mike steps back, still watching her. His spirits remain high. Then he bends over, gently shakes her, and says, "Cass, wake up. It's time to go."

In her sleep, she shrugs him off.

"We don't have all night. We should go now." He shakes her again, this time with a little more force.

The second try does the trick. While her head is faced away, her eyes open. She pulls the bed cover close to her chin and then closes her eyes.

"Cass, don't do this. It's time to go."

Her eyes open wide. Then she turns to face Mike. Shock covers her face.

Mike puts his finger to his lips, "Shh, no noise." He points the gun her way. "Get up. We're leaving."

"What are …?"

Mike prevents her from finishing the sentence. "I said no noise." He tilts his head to the side and waves the revolver. "Get something to put on. It's raining a little outside."

Cass ignores him. "What are you doing here?"

"You're not making it easy. Just do what I tell you to do."

"Get the hell out of my bedroom!"

"Don't yell at me. Get out of bed now, and put something on. We're leaving."

"I'll do whatever I want! Now get the hell out of here! You're insane!"

He feels his body tense up as anger grows. "It's not the time to discuss that."

Her voice is louder and she is now incensed. "I'm not going anyplace with you!"

He feels his temper intensify. "Shh! How many times do I have to tell you?" He nudges her side with the revolver. "You will come with me!"

Cass' pulse speeds up. Then it dawns on her that Charles is not in bed with her. She looks around and then back to Mike. "Where's Charles? What have you done to him?"

He forces himself to settle down, but it is only a little and for a short time. "He's not around. This is how it was meant to be, always."

"I'm not going anyplace with you! Now, get out!"

A mixture of impatience and anger return, "Cass, you're making this harder on yourself." He reaches to grab her out of bed.

"Get your hands off me!" She squirms away from his grasp.

"If you don't come with me I'll put a bullet in your head. If I can't have you then no one will. I'll take Scarlet Rose. She's my daughter. It's up to you. I don't know how to say it any simpler."

It takes her about five seconds to decide. Slowly Cass gets out of bed and walks towards a closet. She quickly changes into something casual all the while trying to come up with a plan to overcome Mike.

He calms down a little. "That's what I'm talking about. It wasn't that hard. Now, let's visit Scarlet Rose."

For a fraction of second Cass wants to charge him, to knock the gun out of his hand and topple him over. The urge lasts a short time after she realizes she would be quickly overcome.

"After you," Mike points the revolver towards the bedroom door. "Lead the way."

Cass suddenly feels weak and light headed. She thinks she might lose her balance so she reaches out to the wall to steady herself. She tells herself not to collapse, not here, not now. She has to go through with it and not leave her daughter behind.

She slowly walks towards her daughter's bedroom with Mike close behind. Halfway there, she gets a surge of energy. She quickly pivots on one foot and takes a wild swing at Mike. Her action is clumsy and uncoordinated. Mike easily grabs her arm.

"Don't ever try that again! Now get moving!" He releases his grip on her arm and then shoves her forward.

Cass gives it one more try to stop him. With teeth clenched, she turns around abruptly. Her fingers are positioned to claw at his face. She lets out a loud scream.

Mike dodges the attack by stepping aside. With his left hand he punches her in the stomach.

Cass lets out a groan and falls to the floor.

"Get up or I'll shoot you where you are."

She slowly gets on one knee and then fully stands. Her face is wiped out.

"Get going."

Cass turns to Mike, "Why are you doing this?" Her voice is without hope.

He ignores her question. "Just get going. Wake Scarlet Rose and tell her to get dressed."

She cannot think of any other option at the moment, so she heads for her daughter's bedroom.

Cass steps inside first. Mike is a few feet behind and the gun is firmly held in his right hand.

Scarlet Rose lays in bed, covers pulled tightly against her face. Her eyes are frightened. "What's going on? I heard you scream."

Cass' smile is weak and her voice is unsettled. "Honey, we've got to go." She looks at her daughter who looks scared and confused. "I'm sorry about this, but you've got to trust me."

She repeats, "What's going on?" She does not notice Mike in the background.

Mike steps forward. His voice is firm and deadly sounding. "Do as your mother says. It's the best for all of us."

Scarlet Rose momentarily stares at Mike and then looks at her mother. "Where's dad?"

"Don't worry about anything, please. We've got to go now." Cass tries to keep her voice under control but the quivering sound is obvious to everyone. "Please," she pleads.

A voice behind Mike surprises everyone. The sound is terse and to the point, nothing anyone present has heard before. "Get out of my house!"

Mike turns to face Charles. His dark brown eyes assess the man standing just a few feet away. There is something different about Charles than just the sound of his voice

231

or the look in his eyes that upsets Mike. He remains motionless for a short time, and then Mike lifts his gun in the direction of Charles. "Don't get in the way."

Charles does not hear a single word from Mike. The part of his brain that oversees his conscious behavior is asleep. It is the other part of his brain that is now in charge, the part that deals with developed patterns such as basic survival instincts. His engine is set in automatic. He is in a fight mode right now, and logic or reasoning cannot override his current mental state.

"I don't want to pull the trigger, but I will if I have to. So, get out of our way, we're leaving." Mike closely watches Charles, keeping an eye on any sudden move.

While Charles is an average sized man and out of shape, he is not afraid. His current mental state of sleep walking has blocked off all feelings, only habitual patterns exist at the moment. His physical strength is average under ordinary conditions, but this situation is anything but ordinary and his power has superman force.

Scarlet Rose lets out a scream, frightened what might happen, "Dad!"

Cass yells at Mike, "Don't do it!"

Charles slowly moves close to Mike.

Mike points the revolver at Charles' head, and threatens, "Back off or I'll kill you."

It is as if Charles knows exactly how to defend himself from an aggressor, as if he has practiced the moves over and over again to prepare for this exact situation.

"I gave you the chance." Mike is about to squeeze the trigger but Charles is too quick.

Charles grabs Mike by the throat with his right hand

and then securely clamps his left hand alongside to make it impossible for Mike to wiggle free.

Mike struggles but manages to get off one round.

The bullet grazes the temple of Charles but does not stop him.

The gun stays in Mike's hand as he takes a swipe at Charles with the weapon. The blow is incidental to harming Charles. Mike then finds the strength to knee Charles in the groin. This time, the kick between the legs is sufficient to loosen Charles' grip on Mike.

Charles falls backward.

"You fucking fucker, I'll kill you." Mike points the gun towards Charles. "You piece of crap." He squeezes off one shot that hits Charles in the shoulder.

Charles' body jumps back on the bullet's impact but not nearly sufficient to put him away for good. Charles staggers to his feet, eyes dead in appearance but focuses on this opponent. Robotically he takes steps to get closer to Mike.

Mike fires off another round, this time it hits Charles in the other shoulder.

Charles keeps coming forward.

"Who the fuck are you?" Mike is about to fire off a fourth bullet but this time Charles is too close to Mike.

Charles is too powerful and this time too quick. He grips Mike's throat. It is more firm and harder than before. Charles keeps an unyielding hold on Mike.

Mike tries to wiggle free. When that doesn't work, he tries to slam the gun into Charles' skull. It is all useless. Mike's arms go limp and he no longer tries to fight back. His entire body stops moving.

Charles releases his grip.

Mike's body falls to the floor.

Cass stays put for a while, paralyzed from the battle between her husband and former lover. Then her brain recovers. She rushes to her husband's side. She tightly holds onto him.

Scarlet Rose remains curled up in bed, too afraid to make a move. Her mind will not allow her to figure anything out right now.

Cass' moves waken Charles from the sleep walk condition. He has no recollection what he has done to the man whose intention was to take his family away from him. He recognizes Cass holding onto him, and then spots his daughter in bed. He calls out to her, "Scarlet Rose, come here. Everything is OK."

Cass looks her way, and then pulls Charles alongside their daughter. They remain clenched in each other's arms.

CHAPTER 8

A voice wakens them.

Charles lies securely strapped in a uniquely designed bed equipped with leg, arm, and body straps to prevent him from escaping or harming himself or others. The hospital room is in the section of St. Claire's General Hospital dedicated to temporarily care for mentally-at-risk patients before they are released from care, assigned to another section of the Hospital, or else transferred to another hospital that specializes in mental care. Cass and Scarlet Rose are each sprawled on small separate cots a few feet away from him.

He slowly shifts his eyes around the room trying to get acquainted with the surroundings. Little by little he remembers where he is. He looks weary and frightened. He smacks his lips but fails to bring together enough energy to call out. He never imagined his life would turn out this way.

Cass takes her time to sit up. She too looks tired and scared. The accumulation of unexpected events over the past few months has taken a toll on her. She looks at her daughter.

While Scarlet Rose's eyes are open, she feels more secure in hugging a pillow than in making a move to get out of bed. She, as well, is worried, but mostly, she is confused.

A hospital volunteer wheels a cart into the room that contains coffee, tea, juice and fresh fruit. She puts on the best smile she knows how to share some cheer and to change the somber mood. "Good morning to everyone."

Charles manages to ask the volunteer, "When am I going to get out of these straps?"

"I don't know. I'm only a volunteer." She keeps a cheerful look on her face.

"They're making me crazy." As soon as he mentions the word crazy, he figures he has said too much.

Cass moves to his side. "I'll ask a nurse or doctor to unfasten these straps. You're not going anyplace without me and your daughter." She smiles at her husband as she leans over to kiss him.

"I can do that. I can ask someone about it." The volunteer is eager to help.

Cass looks her way. "Would you, please. That would be very helpful."

Charles reconsiders. "Why bother?"

Cass looks at Charles with confusion.

"I'm in so much trouble as it is now. Maybe everyone's better off if I stay here for the rest of my life."

Tears come to Cass' eyes. "Don't you dare talk that way. You'll be out of here in a short time, and everything will be back to the way it was."

He smiles at her. "I love you so much."

Scarlet Rose is now by the side of her parents. "I just

want all of this to be over with." She hugs her mother and then gently touches her father's hand.

Moments later a short woman in a white uniform enters the room. "I see everyone is up." Doctor Oshawa moves towards Charles. "How do you feel today?"

"I'd feel a whole lot better if these damn straps were gone."

"I can do that." Doctor Oshawa removes all bindings. "Yes, I'm sure that's better."

"What's the verdict?"

"Mr. Westfield, I'm sure you know what you've done," Doctor Oshawa says but does not wait for a response. "You killed a man while you were mentally asleep but physically awake. In other words you were sleepwalking." She hesitates and then goes on. "We actually refer to what you experienced as a sleep terror."

Cass looks at her daughter and glances at her husband before she talks. "Doctor, we've known for a while that Charles sleepwalks when he is anxious. He's been through a lot these past few months but we thought his medication was working fine." She frowns, looks more worried than before.

"Yes, I've reviewed his medical record."

Scarlet Rose chimes in, "I didn't know that. Why didn't you tell me?" She glances back and forth between her parents.

Charles lets out a slow breath of air. "I guess we thought it was best not to worry you. We're sorry. I guess we should have said something to you."

Scarlet Rose turns to the doctor. "What else should I know about my father?"

Doctor Oshawa smiles. "While I appreciate you

wanting to know about your father's medical background, it is your father and mother that I need to talk with. Certainly you can stay here, but, from a privacy and ethical perspective, I am duty bound to talk directly to them."

"Whatever, I'm not leaving." Scarlet Rose folds her arms over her chest. "And I'm listening."

"Doctor, please go on," Cass asks.

"A sleep terror is different than a dream and it is also different than sleepwalking. For those who experience sleep terrors, their brains shut down, like a power outage. They mentally black out except for the most basic neurological links but their bodies are relatively unaffected."

"Like a zombie?" Scarlet Rose asks.

Doctor Oshawa ignores the comparison to the flesh eating fictional monster. "People with sleep terrors do return as normal functioning human beings." She looks around at them to determine if anything is making sense.

Charles picks up on the purpose of the doctor's hesitation. "Go on, I understand," he says.

"Yes, I'm following you, too," Cass agrees, yet she is unwilling to share with others the previous research she's done on the subject.

Doctor Oshawa looks at Scarlet Rose, "OK so far?"

"Yes," Scarlet Rose answers.

"When someone experiencing a sleep disorder feels threatened, that person either fights or flights. But the important thing to remember here is that the fight or flight is based on that person's previously learned habits that are associated with whatever is going on at that time."

Charles asks, "I don't get that part. Can you give an example?"

Doctor Oshawa nods her head. "People have jumped off of a roof when they believed someone was chasing them, because they believed the only way to escape was to jump off the roof. Some people have harmed animals because they thought the animal was going to attack them." She looks at Scarlet Rose, and then to Cass and finally to Charles.

"Is this genetic?" Charles asks.

"Good question. The answer is we don't know."

"What's going to happen to me now?" Charles grabs hold of Cass' hand as he looks at Doctor Oshawa.

"I can give you medication to help control the sleep terrors, but I can't guarantee if it will work to completely rid you of it. There's no operation known now that could cure it, so that's out of the question. I can recommend professional counseling which in my opinion has the best chance of minimizing the chances of any reoccurrence, but that too is not a one hundred percent guarantee."

Cass takes a deep breath and then lets the air flow out into open space. "So you're saying there is no assurance anything will work. Is that it?" Without consciously thinking about it she squeezes Charles hand.

"Yes, that's what I'm saying."

There is dead silence in the room for a short time.

Then, Doctor Oshawa adds to the conversation. "There's something else you need to worry about."

Charles frowns her way and then glances at Cass. "What?"

"The police, they're going to want to talk with you

once I release you from the hospital and probably even earlier."

Ω Ω Ω Ω Ω

The Immaculate Conception Church looks the same way it did thirty years ago, cathedral looking architecture with stained-glass windows, and several brick stairs leading to two large wooden front doors.

Charles stands at the Church's entrance, hesitates at first but finally makes his way inside. It has been a while since he has been inside a place of workshop of any kind.

He looks around and then takes a seat at the back. The silence within the Church is comforting to him, a place where he can freely think about his troubles. The appearance and smell of candles burning further settles him down. He notices several people standing in two lines alongside a common wall. There is a compartment where each person enters and remains for a few minutes before exiting. He knows these people are confessing their sins to a Catholic Priest. He tells himself he needs someone to talk with, to get things off his chest, so he moves to stand in line along with the others.

Fifteen minutes pass before it is his turn to enter the small space. He hesitates to wonder if it is the right thing to do. About to leave the Church entirely, he feels something pull him back into the line. He steps forward. He has no idea what to expect from the experience.

Now inside the small compartment he kneels and then sees a small screen appear at head level. He is not sure what to do so he says, "I'm not a Catholic. I'm not sure I know why I'm here."

"God does not discriminate. God loves everyone." The soft voice is soothing and comforting. "Tell me, what is troubling you?"

Charles clears his throat. Nerves begin to announce their presence. He rubs his eyes and lets out a puff of air. "I need to talk with you."

"Very well." The priest waits for Charles to continue.

"I'm very nervous right now."

"There is no need to worry. You can speak freely to God who understands all."

"This is not easy to say, it's very personal."

"Whatever you say is between you and God."

"I've cheated on my wife and I'm afraid to tell her." He begins to cry. "I'm sorry. I shouldn't have done it."

While the Priest is not able to identify the man confessing the sin, he has heard similar confessions before. "Do you resolve to sin no more and to ask God for forgiveness?"

Charles gets up and is about to run away. "I shouldn't have come here."

"No," says the Priest. "Please, do not go. Stay calm."

Something in the Priest's voice makes Charles waver.

The Priest's voice is gentle. "You have my solemn word. This is between you and God."

Charles feels his stomach tighten into a knot.

"You've come to God for forgiveness."

Charles senses some loosening of the stomach spasm. "What do I do?"

The Priest raises his shoulders, although the move is

not noticeable by Charles. "Why are you afraid to tell your wife?"

"I think she'll take our child and leave me. I couldn't stand losing them."

"But if you keep your secret to yourself, you believe she'll never know what you've done, is that it?"

Charles nods his head, although the move is only noticeable to him. "That's the idea."

"You would have to keep the secret forever, and that's a long-long time."

It does not take Charles long to interpret the Priest's comment. "I see what you mean."

Stillness returns for a short time.

Charles breaks the silence. "You've done this many times before, haven't you?"

"After a while, you get pretty good at anticipating and understanding. It's all about practice." The Priest smiles to himself.

Charles straightens his body and then twists his head. He hears a popping sound from unloosening a few bones in his neck. "I'm sorry if I've wasted your time."

"No, no waste of my time. Is there something more you'd like to talk about with God?"

"Nothing else. I think I'll go."

"Shall we return to your revolve not to commit the sin again and to ask for God's forgiveness?"

"I'm not Catholic."

"I know, you've said that before. And I said it doesn't matter. Do you revolve not to commit the sin again, and to ask for God's forgiveness?"

Charles' voice is humble. "Yes."

"Are you familiar with the prayer, Act of Contrition?"

"No."

"That's OK." The priest pauses. "Blessed are those with sorrow which comes from the realization that he has offended God, who is infinitely good. Blessed are those with grief for they shall be comforted. May God forgive and be with you forever. You may leave and go in peace."

Charles suddenly realizes what he has to do next. He leaves the Church.

Ω Ω Ω Ω Ω

The ring of the door bell makes Charles flinch. He asks Cass, "Are you expecting anyone?"

She shakes her head, "No, are you?"

"No." He hesitates. Finally, he stands and moves towards the front door. He feels mixed emotions of angst and relief. He wonders if he should have ignored the interruption and told her about the sexual relationship with Denise. It is too late now.

The bell rings again. "Open up, this is the police."

Charles turns towards Cass. "The police?"

She is surprised.

"Just a moment." Charles turns toward the front door. His heart begins to pound.

After a few seconds he opens the front door. Standing before him are two familiar police detectives, Detectives Briley and Cardinale.

"Hello Mr. Westfield, do you remember us?" Cardinale asks the first question.

Startled, he manages to answer. "Yes, of course. What can I do for you?"

Briley takes over, "Can we come in?"

"Who is it?" Cass asks while remained seated on the couch.

"The two detectives who were at the Hospital."

Cass stands and then steps forward until she reaches the front door. "I thought they were all through with questioning you?"

"Hello Mrs. Westfield," Cardinale says.

"What are you doing here?"

"We'd like to come in to talk with your husband again."

"Do you know what this is about?" Cass turns towards Charles.

"No."

Briley decides to cut to the chase. "We have a warrant for your arrest, Mr. Westfield, for the murder of Mr. Michael Aviara. You have the right to remain …"

Charles and Cass no longer consciously listen to the legal rights being explained. Before they realize it, Charles is handcuffed and taken to the unmarked police vehicle outside their residence.

Cass shouts, "I'm coming." Then she grabs her cell phone to call her neighbor. "Iris, Charles needs a defense attorney right away. Can you call Joe to get someone from his firm to meet us at the police station immediately?"

Briley is about to confirm the protocol with Cardinale. However, she says, "I guess it won't hurt if she rides along."

Ω Ω Ω Ω Ω

The ride to the police department is nerve-racking. Cass has ever been inside a police vehicle, whereas Charles has once before. They feel as if their world is crumbling into sand.

"I'm so sorry about this." She touches his hand. "I'm sorry."

His eyes have the worried look. "You haven't done anything wrong. It's been me, all me."

She frowns with greater concern. "No, there are things I need to tell you, things that I've kept hidden from you. It's eating me up insides."

"No, there isn't anything you need to say. Don't try to make it easy on me. I'm the one who's got secrets, not you. You're going to be better off without me."

"What about our daughter? She needs you as her father."

"I can't …" His voice trails off before he can finish the thought.

Cass squeezes his hand. "Sometimes things build up inside me that I can't seem to hold in. Then, all of a sudden, they're gone and I conveniently forget about it."

Charles turns away. "I know what you mean. I understand. It happens to me as well."

"So, you can't give up and you can't let go of what we have." Cass grabs his arm. "Look at me, please."

"You're being kind to me. I can't face you."

"It's not a question of kindness, you know that."

"Then what, what is it?"

"It's a matter of us trusting each other regardless of what we've done to each other. Can you forgive me?"

Charles turns to face her. "Forgive you, for what? It's me who needs forgiveness."

It is now Cass' turn to look away. She sees her reflection in the door window and realizes how terrified she looks. She lets out a frightened moan.

His voice breaks up with emotion as he asks, "What's the matter?"

The police vehicle suddenly stops with a jolt to cut short their conversation.

Cardinale twists her body to face Charles and Cass. "We're here. Mrs. Westfield, he's coming with us while you can take a seat in the waiting area."

Cass hugs Charles as if it is the last time they will be together. "I called Iris before we left the house to get a hold of Joe to send us a defense attorney from his office."

Ω Ω Ω Ω Ω

Charles visibly shakes his head sideways, his body fully controlled by nerves. "You don't really think I meant to kill him, do you?"

Briley says, "We're only going by the evidence. Your wife and daughter witnessed it."

"But I didn't mean to. You've read the doctor's report. I was not aware of what I was doing. I have a medical problem."

Briley looks at Cardinale, "Yeah, we read the report." He turns to face Charles, "Something about sleepwalking."

Charles' stomach sinks. He realizes they don't care much about the medical information. All they want is a conviction. "You don't understand." He pauses and then repeats it again, "You don't understand, I have a medical problem that's not curable!"

Ω Ω Ω Ω Ω

Someone new enters the room. "I'm Oliver Shackleford. I am representing Mr. Westfield. I want to talk with my client alone. Please excuse us." Shackleford immediately places on the table his briefcase, ignoring whatever response may come from the Detectives.

Cardinale says to Briley, "No surprise, he's lawyered up. Let's go."

Once Shackleford is alone with Charles he gets right to work. "I'm a partner at the same firm Joe Mesa is with. He told me you need a defense attorney."

Charles says, "Yes, that's right. I knew I could count on him."

"My specialty is defense work. But at the same time, don't get overconfident that this will be easy. I'm not yet familiar with your specific case, and defense work is not easy. Know what I mean?"

"Yes, of course. But it was self-defense. My family told me he had a gun pointed at my head. Who's investigating the fact that he had a gun? Further, I was not in control of my actions. There's medical evidence to prove it!"

"There is evidence and there is evidence. In my legal experience most medical evidence usually consists of research data that implies, suggests, and hypothesizes. I suspect the District Attorney will find research scientists and medical practitioners who have an opposite opinion of whatever your doctor says. That's just how it works."

"What about self-defense? He came into my home with a gun to take away my family"

"Certainly that shows motive on his part and self-defense on your part." He puffs out a breath of air. "I'm sure this case is more complex than his motive, your self-defense and medical evidence."

"I don't like what you're saying."

"Mr. Westfield, if I were in your shoes neither would I. But we've got to do our best to convince a judge or a jury of your innocence. Do you understand me?"

"Yes, I think I do."

"That's good for now. You've got to tell me everything, even if it is uncomfortable or embarrassing. That's the only way I can help you."

Charles pauses. "I don't know where to start."

"Mr. Mesa told me a little about your unemployment situation and how badly you felt during that time. Let's start there and take me up to now."

"Is that all he said?"

"Yes, but you're going to tell me everything, and I do mean everything. Let's get going."

"OK, I'll start with my wife's college class reunion."

"I'm listening." Shackleford takes out a note pad. "I'm going to take notes."

Ω Ω Ω Ω Ω

Three hours later, Charles says, "That's about it. I'm sure the detectives have their notes."

"I'm sure they do. I'll be talking with your doctor and I'm going to be looking at the video. Is there anything I should be focusing on?"

"It will definitely prove she was the aggressor."

"Anything else?"

"No, I can't think of anything else at the moment."

"Alright then, I'm going to review my notes with you

now. Stop me at anytime if you think I've misunderstood something or left out something." Shackleford looks at his notes. "You said you were feeling down in the dumps from being unemployed for close to six months and thought that your relationship with your wife was a bit strained. When she told you of her plans to attend her college class reunion you were a little miffed, perhaps jealous, but kept those feelings to yourself. When she returned home after the reunion, you sensed something different about her but decided against asking her any questions. Then her classmate, Mike Aviara, called you to say he could help you find a job. That conversation eventually led to you getting hired by First Floor Solar. That is when and where you met Denise Cameon, and then the ensuing one-time sexual affair. You told your boss, Mr. Alan Jessup, about the situation and the both of you agreed to make a copy of the video and to destroy the laptop hard drive. Then the detectives informed you that Cameon was killed. At first you were the prime suspect, but later, they changed their minds. You've also said a few times that you do not believe your wife knows of the affair with Cameon and you do not suspect she has had or is having an affair with anyone. You were shot three times by Mr. Aviara. One bullet grazed your skull while two penetrated your body. After you strangled Aviara you told me your wife said to you that she believed Aviara was obsessed with her, something that probably dating back to their college days. She told you she believed that Aviara's plan was to take her and your daughter away from you, even if it meant killing you. Finally, you don't remember anything that happened that early morning when Aviara broke into your home." Shackleford looks up from his notes, "Does that sum it up?"

Charles stares at Shackleford. His eyes are glazed over. "I don't know if I want to go through with this."

Shackleford's face is tight with shock. "What are you talking about?"

"I can't allow my family to know anything about Denise. It will ruin my marriage. I'm going to confess to killing Aviara and hope you can get me a reduced sentence due to my medical problem."

Shackleford is not giving up on his client. He takes in a deep breath and sits back in his chair to think of something to say. Then he leans forward, and places both hands flat on the desk. "Look. It would be a whole lot easier if the Cameon situation never took place, if you had told your wife and daughter about Cameon, if Aviara hadn't tried to take away your family at gun point, and if you hadn't strangled him to death. But, let's be realistic, it is what it is. My strong legal recommendation is to get through with the legal part of the situation and then deal with whatever you decide to say to your family. I'll handle the legal part if your handle your personal part. What do you say, do we have a deal?" He waits to hear an answer.

Charles keeps quiet for a little longer, looks away and then back towards Shackleford. "I'm so sorry for what I've done, all of it. It was stupid of me to have the affair with her and then to keep it quiet. I should have told Cass about it immediately. She would have understood."

Shackleford looks on, not surprised with his client's reaction. He waits, anticipating another response soon. When it does not come he decides to say something. "The case against you is for the murder of Mr. Aviara, nothing about you and Cameon. I intend to object to the District Attorney trying to put into evidence anything not directly related to the murder of Aviara. I believe that whatever was going on between you and Cameon is not relevant to this specific case. In other words, I will do my best to suppress anything about Cameon as well as anything else that has no direct connection to the murder of Aviara. The only thing that matters in this case is that Mike Aviara broke into your home and, at gun point, tried to kidnap your family. You acted to protect your family. That's it, nothing else."

"So my family won't hear about Denise and me?"

"What I'm telling you is that I will do my best to prevent information about you and her be entered into evidence. That's my promise."

"What about my medical problem?"

"I'll try to get that put into evidence, but I've got to think about that some more. I'm not sure it will be compelling enough. It might even contradict the self-defense claim."

Charles waits a few seconds before he replies. He clears his throat and then answers. "I'll tell them everything after it is all over."

Shackleford tilts his head to the side, uncertain of the answer. "I'm sure you will. Are you telling me you agree to proceed with the case as I've just described?"

"Yes, let's go ahead. I'll own up to everything with Cass and Scarlet Rose after the case is decided."

Shackleford's blue eyes are intense as he stares at Charles. He extends his hand. "Let's shake on it."

Charles seals the deal when he reaches over to grab Shackleford's hand. "How's this going to proceed?"

"First of all you've got to understand that criminal procedure is adversarial. It's them against us. The District Attorney is going to try to put into evidence everything that helps their side and to prevent us from putting into evidence anything that hurts their side. I'm going to do the same thing to advance our case and prevent them from putting into evidence anything that will harm us. The judge acts as an impartial referee between them and us. Do you understand?" He waits for a response.

"Yes I do. I'm as ready as I'll ever be."

"You've been read your Miranda rights and have already been arrested by the police. You now have counsel by me. This means you are not to say anything to anyone except when I am physically present. I will also advise you on whether to answer a question or be quiet. This is important, very important. Do you understand?"

Another head nod from Charles.

"The next step is going to be an arraignment where you will be charged with the specific crime and be given an opportunity to enter a plea. We will enter a non-guilty plea. Then there are several other steps that I don't want to overwhelm you with such as a preliminary hearing, pretrial motions, the actual trial, the verdict and sentencing if there is one. This is going to be stressful for you and your family. You've got to stay strong throughout it all. I'll not give up on you but I need the same commitment from you as well. We're in this together. Do you understand?"

"Yes, I do."

"I've got a preliminary idea about what to do next, but there's some further research to be done. I might not see you for a few days after the arraignment. Don't worry. All it means is that I'm looking into something."

"What are you thinking about doing?"

"It's too early to tell you anything, but trust me that I know what I'm doing."

Ω Ω Ω Ω Ω

Inside Judge Parker's chambers, Oliver Shackleford and Assistant District Attorney Kimberly Hoffman argue as a court reporter takes notes.

"Judge Parker, this is preposterous, filing a motion to dismiss!"

"Miss Hoffman, quite the contrary. Mr. Shackleford has the legal right to file a motion to dismiss on behalf of his client, and you know that to be within the law. He has filed the appropriate papers that state the agreed upon facts are insufficient to establish his client's guilt. Do I need to review in more detail with you what is required to file a motion to dismiss?"

"No. That's not necessary." Hoffman swallows and then continues. "I do not believe the State's self-defense law applies here. I have a preponderance of evidence to prove that Mr. Westfield did not solely act in self-defense. He had motive. He was covering up a sexual affair with a business associate and …"

Shackleford interrupts, "Whatever alleged sexual affair he may have had with someone is not the issue here."

Hoffman counters, "It is pertinent because it is indicative of his overall pathetic character, someone who is irresponsible that includes but is not limited to keeping his marriage vows."

It is Shackleford's turn. "Marriage and murder

are separate issues. They do not belong in the same conversation."

Hoffman is about to rebut, but Parker takes control of the debate. "Settle down everyone. We shall follow the prescribed protocol for this filing. First, Mr. Shackleford will present his side, and then Miss Hoffman will have her turn. We will continue that process until I am satisfied all relevant information has been offered. The arguments will be presented in a civil manner. Miss Martinez, the court reporter, will take notes. Do I make myself clear?" He looks for acknowledgments from both attorneys. "Fine, that is settled. Mr. Shackleford, you're up."

Shackleford turns towards Parker. "Thank you, Judge Parker." He glances at a piece of paper in his hands and then turns to look at Parker. "The State's self-defense law applies to Mr. Charles Westfield. The law states that any person who, with good reason, uses force in self-defense is immune from criminal prosecution. Mr. Westfield believed he and his family were threatened by Mr. Aviara, the man who broke into his house and attempted to kidnap his wife and young daughter. Mr. Aviara held a gun to my client's head and threatened to kill him. He actually shot my client three times. Mr. Westfield acted out of fear rather than anger. He was protecting himself and his family from Aviara's threat. He is statutorily immune to a trial, should never have been arrested, detained, or charged. Further, the information about his alleged sexual affair is not relevant to this case. Therefore, Judge Parker, I believe Charles Westfield acted out of self-defense and therefore all charges against him be dismissed. Thank you." He keeps his look directed at Judge Parker.

"OK, Miss Hoffman, it's your turn. Let me hear what the A. D. A. has to say."

"Thank you, Judge Parker. Mr. Westfield's affair is not alleged and it directly pertains to his actions towards Mr. Aviara. It shows a pattern of out of control and reckless behavior, first with the adulterous sexual affair with Denise Cameon, and then with the brutal, vicious, and intentional murder of Mike Aviara. It all started when Mr. Westfield was laid off from work. He was miserable during the six month period of unemployment. His wife tried to uplift his spirits but that failed. She asked him to join her at her college class reunion, but he refused, he wanted to be left alone, to feel sorry for himself. I interviewed some of their classmates who attended the college class reunion. One in particular told me she and Mr. Aviara flirted heavily during that time, and further she believed it was highly likely Mrs. Westfield had at least one sexual affair with Mr. Aviara, perhaps more. They obviously began to intentionally rekindle their intimate relationship from their college days. I suspect she wanted out of her marriage to be with Mr. Aviara, and I suspect Aviara was willing to go along because he was in love with her. Then, Mr. Westfield had an affair with the Human Resources Director, Miss Denise Cameon, of First Floor Solar, the company he hired into. I might add that Mr. Aviara was responsible for getting him the interview and eventually the job offer. Mr. Westfield should have regarded Mr. Aviara as a friend, not a threat. Knowing that the sexual affair with Miss Cameon would eventually come out, Mr. Westfield reluctantly told the investigative detectives about the sexual affair but claimed the woman came on to him. I have the video of the entire affair that he claimed was recorded by her. I've seen the video. Whether she came onto him or the other way around is purely speculative, and whether she recorded it or he recorded it for his own perverse pleasure is also speculative. Shortly after the sexual affair, Cameon was found murdered in the desert. Mr. Westfield said he was surprised about her death, and as I've previously stated, he initially denied having sex with her but later recanted. I believe that Mrs. Westfield and Mr. Aviara agreed to take her daughter and run away together. Further we believe that when Mr. Westfield found out about their plans he was enraged and set out to kill Aviara. He waited for the exact moment, calculating how he would kill Mr. Aviara. Mr. Westfield had it all meticulously planned out. When Mr. Aviara showed up at their home, Mr. Westfield found it to be the perfect opportunity to kill him. He acted out of rage and anger. He knew exactly what he was doing. He knowingly killed Mr. Aviara. Mr. Shackleford might claim that his client acted out of self-defense, but we all know differently. Thank you."

"OK, Mr. Shackleford, it's your turn."

"I've heard the A. D. A. state alleged facts that are merely speculative. She has put forward her personal but unfounded beliefs. She has a way of choosing unparalleled superlatives to describe situations that rival some of the best mystery writers. So, now is the time to be straightforward and to tell the truth. I will set the record straight. My client admits he was down in the dumps during the six ·months of unemployment. I mean, who wouldn't? He also acknowledges that he saw no reason to join his wife at her college reunion. And lastly, he was both surprised and pleased when Aviara helped him get the job at First Floor

Solar. However, all the talk about his wife having an affair with Aviara is unfounded. Who are the witnesses? This is the first time I've heard of someone from the reunion who claims she saw Mrs. Westfield and Mr. Aviara flirt. Did Mrs. Westfield confess to having an affair? I don't think so. Certainly we can't ask Aviara for the obvious reason. My client never suspected his wife was unfaithful to him. My client is terribly upset about his one-time affair, but there is absolutely no connection between that affair with the death of Aviara, or with the death of Cameon. In fact, I believe Mr. Aviara tried to deposit money into my client's bank account to look as if my client was being paid off for Cameon's murder. My client was thoroughly investigated about the unfortunate murder of this woman and was not found to be involved in any way. The investigative detectives concluded that the woman's death was meant to look like a suicide but in fact the evidence suggests it was a mob hit. And there is another important point that has not been brought up." He looks at Hoffman and then back to Parker. "Mr. Aviara had ties to organized crime. Miss Hoffman knows that, but she failed to mention it. We further believe that Mr. Aviara paid Miss Cameon to seduce my client to make it easy for him to take Mrs. Westfield away from my client. Then Mr. Aviara had Miss Cameon murdered in order to place the blame on Mr. Westfield, which would then open up his chances to be with Mrs. Westfield, the woman he was obsessed with."

Hoffman shouts, "None of this is relevant and there is no evidence to prove it!"

"Miss Hoffman, you will abide by my rules." Parker glares at her, and then faces Shackleford. "Please continue."

"Finally, it is a fact that Mr. Westfield suffers from sleep terrors, a form of sleepwalking, when he is not aware of what he is doing. This illness is not totally understood, but for a number of people who experience them, violent actions are part of it. There is scientific research to support this claim. If Mr. Westfield was suffering from a sleep terror at the time of Mr. Aviara's death, my client was not consciously aware of his actions."

Hoffman interrupts again, "It is absurd to believe that Mr. Westfield was asleep as he choked Mr. Aviara to his death, in full view of his family. The research Mr. Shackleford mentions is not conclusive."

Judge Parker glares at Hoffman. "Have you already forgotten what I've said about following protocol?"

Hoffman says, "I'm sorry Judge Parker, but Mr. Shackleford is scripting a story that is utterly false."

"I trust you'll let me figure that out." Then Parker turns to Shackleford, "This is your last opportunity Mr. Shackleford. Do you have anything else to add?"

"No," replies Shackleford.

Parker looks at Hoffman, "Does the A. D. A. have anything else to add, this is your last opportunity?"

"No," replies Hoffman.

Parker tilts back in his chair. "Return to my chambers in two days at 10:00 AM for my decision."

Ω Ω Ω Ω Ω

Two days later, Judge Parker speaks to Shackleford and Hoffman as the same court reporter, Miss Martinez, takes notes. "At first, this case appeared complex but as I reviewed the written motion, my notes, and the court reporter's notes of your presentations, the facts became clear. I congratulate each of you for preparing and explaining your positions. The sexual affair between Mr. Westfield and Miss Cameon, and the sexual affair or affairs between Mrs. Westfield and Mr. Aviara are irrelevant to this case. While sexual affairs with someone other than one's spouse may be offensive to some people, they bear no relevance to Mr. Aviara's murder. So I repeat for emphasis, there is no link between the sexual affairs and the death of Mr. Aviara. The murder of Miss Cameon, while not yet solved, is also not relevant to this particular case. Therefore, all information related to Cameon's murder is irrelevant. While Mr. Aviara may or may not have been affiliated with organized crime is interesting, I find that information to be irrelevant as well. However, the sleepwalking defense is interesting. My research indicates opposing positions on the topic. If sleepwalking was the central issue, then we would have to bring in experts to get a much better understanding. Therefore, Mr. Westfield's medical condition of walking in his sleep is irrelevant to this particular case. So, as I see it, this leaves us with one real issue, the applicability of our State's self-defense law. Here are the relevant facts. Mr. Aviara broke into the Westfield home. According to the testimony of Mrs. Westfield, he tried to kidnap her and her teenage daughter at gun point. Mr. Aviara threatened her husband with the same gun. He shot Mr. Westfield three times, one bullet grazed his skull and two hit his body. Then, Mr. Westfield choked Mr. Aviara. In my final opinion, there is no confusion about the applicability of our State's self-defense law in this case. It is clear to me that it applies. Therefore, the evidence, as presented, demonstrates Mr. Westfield acted in self-defense. I dismiss this case because Mr. Westfield justifiably used force in self-defense. Charles Westfield must be set free."

CHAPTER 9

Outside the restaurant pedestrians busily walk. The noise of the traffic interferes with normal conversations. Charles studies those passing by and then looks at his wife and daughter. He smiles their way and kisses each of them. Then he says, "Let's go in."

A man dressed in a dark suit, white shirt, and black tie stands behind a stand. He smiles their way. He has a French accent. "Good evening. Do you have reservations?"

"Yes, three for 6 PM. The name is Westfield."

The maître d' looks down at the reservation book. "Yes, here it is." He smiles, makes a check mark next to the last name, and then steps away from the stand. "Please follow me. We have a nice quiet table for you."

Cass grabs one arm while Scarlet Rose takes her father's other arm. They proudly follow the man in the black suit.

"Here we are." The maître d' pulls one chair away from the table. "Please." He nods towards Cass.

Once she sits down he moves towards a second chair to repeat the same process for Scarlet Rose.

During this time Charles takes the empty seat.

"A waiter will join you shortly. Bon appetite." He steps back and returns to the stand where a couple patiently waits their turn.

Scarlet Rose is the first to talk. She looks at her father. "This is cool. You're the greatest." She then takes a quick glance around the room.

A young male suddenly appears holding a decanter of water. As with the maître d', he has a French accent. "Pardon me. May I pour you water."

Scarlet Rose takes a good look at him. She feels her pulse beat up a little at the handsome young man. "Merci," she manages to say. She feels her face blush.

"Parlez-vous Français?"

"Un peu."

"Merveilleux." He smiles her way, finishes pouring water into their glasses. Then he says, "Au revoir."

Cass looks at her daughter. "Hmm." She smiles.

"I guess you didn't know I'm worldly." Scarlet Rose flickers her eyebrows as a friendly tease.

"Just don't grow up too fast," her father says. He thinks to himself she will soon be a fully mature woman.

Scarlet Rose shrugs her shoulders. "It's going to happen anyway."

Cass glances between her daughter and husband. Her eyes feel a little wet so she discreetly touches their corners with a finger tip. She desperately wants to tell Charles all about her and Mike, but she cannot pull herself to confessing. The shock of her husband's ordeal and everything associated with it is too overwhelming right now for her to tell a soul. It seems clear to her that her secret is securely locked in an inner vault and the key is hidden away.

Charles struggles with a similar feeling, flipping back and forth about what to do concerning his secret. He too is all worked up inside about what he has concealed and if told to his family what the consequences might be. The emotion he feels inside distort much rationale thinking, but he wearily promises that soon, when he and Cass are alone, he will disclose everything. He does not think he can go on living with the skeleton hidden deep within.

"What are you two thinking about? You seem to be in your own worlds." Scarlet Rose glances back and forth between her parents.

Cass' thoughts are interrupted. "What did you say?" She looks at her daughter.

"Oh, nothing."

Cass is persistent. "Sure you did. I'm sorry but my mind was wandering someplace."

Scarlet Rose takes a sip of water. "I was just wondering when we were going to get the menus. I'm starved." She looks at her father and then glances away.

Charles agrees. "Me too, I'm hungry."

As if on cue, a female waitress with a French accent appears. "Good evening. I'm Lauriane and I'll be your server. Can I offer you something to drink before dinner?"

Ω Ω Ω Ω Ω

Shortly before dawn the next day, Cass wakes up from a sound sleep. She feels a chill in the air so she pulls the covers close up to her chin. Then she rotates her body to the side to snuggle up close to Charles. She is surprised to find him elsewhere. Cass turns towards an opened sliding glass door just off the master bedroom that leads to a balcony. She sits up to focus and sees Charles sitting on a chair outside. "Charles, what are you doing out there?"

There is only silence as a response.

She automatically thinks he is sleepwalking again.

"Yes?" Charles sounds as if he is having trouble breathing. "I've been doing a lot of thinking."

"That's behind us. You were protecting your family in self-defense. Come on back to bed where it's warm."

"The air feels good."

She grabs a robe to pull over her nightgown and walks onto the balcony to sit alongside him."What's troubling you?"

"I can see more clearly now." He shifts his body in the black metal chair.

"What are you talking about?"

"I need more time to get over it."

"Whatever time you need, you should take it. I'm sure it was very stressful. I'll always be by your side."

"I need time to think about the consequences."

"Of course, I understand more than you know."

"You've always understood me more than I've understood myself. You're my foundation, so strong and so sensible."

Cass swallows. She wonders if she has enough strength left to go on with her charade. "And I love you more than words can describe. You are the best husband I could ever have and the best father for Scarlet Rose."

Their conversation is interrupted by the meow of a stray cat just below the balcony.

Charles looks down at the cat and whispers loud

enough for both of them to hear. "All alone and no place to go."

Cass is not sure what to make of the comment so she lets it go. However, the distraction is sufficient for her to change the subject. "Let's get back to bed where it's warmer. I'm getting cold out here."

He turns to face her, and then takes hold of her hands in his. "I promise from this point forward I will be completely honest with you."

The unexpected comment takes her by surprise. She is sure he is referring to the other times when he has sleepwalked and not told her. "And I promise never to hold back anything from you."

He does not pick up on anything beyond her words of a future commitment. "I love you. I was terrified I was going to lose you."

She feels her throat constrict a little but manages to say, "That's never going to happen."

They embrace, kiss each other sweetly on the lips, and return to their bed. They smile at the bedside photo of Charles, Cass, and Scarlet Rose.

— the end —

About the Author

Antonio F. Vianna is a prime example of someone who has re-careered himself. In fact, you might say he wrote the book on it with "Career Management and Employee Portfolio Tool Kit, 3rd edition." He holds a M.M. from Northwestern University's Kellogg Graduate School of Management and a B.S. from Union College. He has been able to re-brand himself from a former U.S. Air Force officer and Human Resources executive to an author and educator. This is his 20th published book since 2003. He has written 5 screenplays that have been adapted from 5 of his novels, and he conducts three popular workshops, *"Re-Careering at Any Age," "How to Write a Book and Get Published,"* and *"How to Write a Screenplay."*

Vianna is frequently a guest on television and radio discussing strategies for re-careering at any age. He is a member of Publishers and Writers of San Diego, Read Local San Diego, and the Military Writers Society of America. He is on-faculty with several San Diego universities. Vianna lives in Carlsbad, Calif. His books are available in paperback and electronically wherever books are sold. For more information about Antonio F. Vianna and his other books, go to his website at <u>www.viannabooks4u.com</u>.

NON-FICTION

Career Management and Employee Portfolio Tool Kit Workbook, 3rd edition (2010) posits that your career is a dynamic process that requires constant reevaluation and fine-tuning as experience dictates. With practical exercises focusing on his model, *Five Sigma of Success*, this *Workbook* helps the first-time job seeker, those reentering the workforce or changing jobs/careers, and those currently employed who seek advancement evaluate who they are, what they want to be, and how to get there. (ISBN: 978-1-4107-1100-7)

In ***Leader Champions: Secrets of Success*** (2004) Vianna and Dr. Mark B. Silber create a dynamic text about your choices for leader champion actions. Their goal focuses on what it means to be a leader in the 21st Century and what some practical techniques used by those who have made it to that exclusive suite. This is a no-nonsense text to stimulate your leadership, human relations, and personal growth competencies. (ISBN: 1-4184-3684-4)

FICTION

A Tale from a Ghost Dance (2003) is Vianna's first novel. The story centers on the title's reference to the ancient Native American ceremonial dance where the spirits of the ancestors are called upon for their wisdom and advice. But, in this tale, it is an Anglo woman executive who has unwanted visionary powers. The protagonist, Victoria, is a high-powered marketing executive who does not accept her gift until she encounters a Native American elder,

Joseph. However, some tribal members resent Victoria. These ensure intra-tribal conflicts as well as mysterious circumstances involving one of her clients that place her life and others in peril. (ISBN: 1-4107-1384-9)

In *The In-ter-view* (2003) Vianna employs some of his professional human resources experiences to turn something as ordinary as a job interview into a life and death drama. While Laura Simmons interviews with Fred Wheeler and Associates, a disgruntled former employee bursts in and takes her and seven others hostage. As the action plays out, each character reveals their true self and demonstrates how each individual reacts under duress. It soon becomes evident if they want to survive the ordeal, this disparate group must become a cohesive force. (ISBN: 1-4107-0876-4)

The backdrop of **Talking Rain** (2004) is a twenty-year-old murder case that sent a man to death row. One evening, however, alone, with no one left to talk with, Lucy Lodine unexpectedly walks into Precinct 21 to break her silence. She confesses to the murder, but is unsuccessful in convincing the authorities that her husband on death row is innocent of the crime. When people who had been involved in the crime start to die, she gets the authority's attention, specifically Detective Jack Bogle. Mix in academic rivalry, problem gambling, an alleged affair, and a callow policewoman with her on-again off-again boyfriend reporter, and you have an incredible topsy-turvy ride. (ISBN: 1-4140-6648-1)

Uncovered Secrets (2005) takes place in a local movie theater. What would you do if your darkest secret was about to be uncovered? Blend in a ghost, the theater's sexy and manipulative employee, the theater's film projectionist, a callous cop, the theater's manager who shows signs of being in a profession too long, a brash young female executive, and an emotionally needy woman. The final secrets are revealed on North County Airport Road. (ISBN: 1-4208-1795-7)

In *Midnight Blue* (2005) after two bodies are exhumed, the police begin to suspect foul play and question their original findings. Were lies purposely told and the real suspects purposely not questioned? Throw into the mix a love affair between a cop and the daughter of the prime suspect, and you have a story you will want to read straight through. (ISBN: 1-4208-6397-5)

Veil of Ignorance (2006) is a suspense novel about Tommy Hogan, an outstanding University educator, whose loneliness and search for happiness gets him embroiled in life and death situations. As his vulnerabilities surface, he easily becomes a target by those seeking revenge, greed, and status at the expense of others. It takes Tommy a while to realize he is being conned, and when he does, he understands that his misguided affection is actually towards the very person who seeks his demise. The face-off at the end helps him remove the veil that shrouds his ignorance. (ISBN: 1-4259-1695-3)

In *Yellow Moon* (2006) one year after the conviction of Jimmy Lupo, a man accused of robbing a bank, Bella Lupo, the daughter of the convicted man reaches out to Ned Francis, a private investigator to dig up evidence that her father had taken a fall and been wrongly imprisoned for the crime. Although the hard-nosed detective is initially skeptical, he eventually believes that her father was in fact a patsy. Although he slams into one dead end after another, the detective never gives up the search for justice. However, he begins to fall in love with the prisoner's daughter, and it seems he is captivated by the daughter's good looks and seductive ways. Is he really convinced of her father's innocence, or is he too much in love to see the real truth? As strange obsessions and lust for power grow, a climactic standoff will shock you. (ISBN: 1-4259-5112-0)

Hidden Dangers (2007) follows a journey into hidden dangers of espionage, revenge, greed, love, and hope. It all starts one night with a strange telephone call to Connie Marz, a Specialty Leasing Manager with a local shopping mall. Drop into the mixture a mysterious mall walker's disappearance, cozy American and Russian government agents spying on one another, an unlikely love relationship, and one person with the courage to put it all to an end. Characters agonize over their self-doubts and pleasure at their misplaced sense of superiorities. It all sounds crazy, and to someone it is. (ISBN: 978-1-4259-9710-6)

In *Haunted Memories* (2007) thirteen-year-old Dave Stagetto goes missing, even though his best boyhood friend, Billy, keeps something a secret. While the small town of Hadley grieves for a short time, Dave's mother falls deeper into depression to the very core of her soul. She suspects something just does not make sense, but is not sure what. Worse of all, the haunted memories, thought to be discarded with time, emerge twenty years later to everyone's surprise. Childhood relationships change as people grow older, often times in strange and surprising ways. The search for the truth shifts between San Diego,

California and Lisbon, Portugal until the terrible secret is unveiled. (ISBN: 978-1-4343-2852-6)

In *Bound and Determined* (2008) Susanne Attrice likes being in control. However, when she unexpectedly becomes pregnant, not sure the identity of the biological father, her life turns upside down. Then, suddenly, her infant child is abducted from the hospital. She suspects who the child snatcher might be, so she now is bound and determined to be reunited with her baby. It proves tougher than she ever imagined. As she begins putting pieces of the puzzle together, she shoves aside those who are willing and able to help her the most. Does she have enough inner strength to go it alone or will she reach out for help? (ISBN: 978-1-4343-7450-9)

Stranger On A Train (2009) is Book 1 of a vampire trilogy. Are there bounds of human behavior that you will not cross, or aren't there? What someone may believe in and subsequently do as acceptable, another may find despicable. Paul Autore, an aspiring novelist, meets Marcus Varro on a train. Later Paul receives two unusual letters from Marcus inviting him to Sanibel Island, Florida, to tutor Anne, Marcus's beautiful daughter. Even before he arrives at the spacious white mansion, Paul suspects something else is up; and when he and Marcus almost die from an automobile accident on their way to the Varro residence, tensions rise even further. Simmering family hatreds heat up that put Paul in the middle. Caught up in things shockingly different than what he has ever written about or experienced, he might have to cross a boundary he never thought he would. Is Paul prepared to go to extreme lengths to protect him? (ISBN: 978-1-4389-1490-9)

The Hiding (2009) is Book 2 of a vampire trilogy. There are places, deep below the earth's surface where vampires exist, unknown to mortals. It is their Hiding place. No one knows for certain their origins, although myths and legends abound. Yet, one thing is for certain. They battle each other to maintain some sort of balance of power among them. This all changes, however, as Anne Varro, a beautiful young woman begins a mysterious transformation to become a hybrid, part human and part vampire. A bitter feud erupts as two clans of vampires fight to claim her as their own. (ISBN: 978-1-4389-6206-1)

The Vampire Who Loved (2009) is Book 3 of a vampire trilogy. As this novel opens, Anne is awakened from a horrifying nightmare. She wonders if the dream is a predictor of events to come. All the while, her enemies, some old and some new, are intent to have their own way … vampires who set in motion seemingly irreversible measures to do away with her. Paul has become the X-factor … his predictability is uncertain. Anne calls upon Vincent Blackfoot, now her closest friend and ally, to help figure out a plan. As the story rushes to a surprising climax, a sudden twist appears. (ISBN: 978-1-4490-2488-8)

Second Son (2010). What if a child's birth order determines the degree of love he receives from his parents? Robert does not receive love and attention from his parents as a young boy, so he turns to the Church to become a Catholic Priest. His moral fiber is turned upside down when his older brother asks for a favor that would violate his sacred vows and cause him to commit an act filled with deceit and lies. (ISBN: 978-1-4490-7473-9)

Unintentional Consequences (2010). Rand Bauge never thought he was simply working for wages when he was employed by the U. S. Government, although there were enough situations that would contradict that notion. He got things done any way he could; usually it was his way. No one seemed to care about the means he used. Questions were rarely asked. Only the results mattered. He and his boss saw eye to eye on their relationship because it worked well for a good long time. Things change when he goes on his own, retirement urged upon him against his wishes. The panic call he gets from his second wife throws him for a loop … something bad has gone wrong at home. He's got to get there fast before it is too late. However, along the way, unintended surprises block his advancement. Who's really out to get him? This might be the biggest test ever. (ISBN: 978-1-4520-6901-2)

Time and Money (2011). He was a bad-tempered young man at 18 and got even surlier as he aged. Then, his life got more complicated. The old man took advantage of others for most of his life. In fact he enjoyed reaping the benefits from the pain he inflicted on others. He figured it was just the way it was, as the Sun rose in the East and set in the West. Then, late in his years, he meets Riley Sullivan, a good natured fellow, someone who perfectly fits into his final scheme to put the last touches on his existence. However, all his ill deeds and future schemes meet up with unexpected guilt as he tries to make amends. (ISBN: 978-1-4634-3945-3)

Unordinary Love. (2012). When Carl joins the Whitaker family as an adopted boy, he is shunned by his older stepbrother Paul and younger stepsister Kay. However, over a short time, Kay's affection toward Carl grows while Paul's animosity with his stepbrother quickly deepens with jealousy. Kay and Carl become locked in a relationship so unrelenting that they become the center of each other's world, and are prepared to cross a boundary they never thought they would. As their teen years turn to young adulthood, unexpected changes occur that put more than just the two of them in life threatening conditions. Who will live on and who will perish is not necessarily a matter of choice, but rather a matter of chance. Their almost unconscious acts seem to turn into their lives' fulfillment. (ISBN: 978-1-4685-4677-4)

Other Titles by Antonio F. Vianna

www.viannabooks4u.com.